JUNIOR WEIGHT TRAINING

AND STRENGTH TRAINING

By Tim Smith

Published By:
The Athletic Institute
200 Castlewood Drive
North Palm Beach, FL 33408
U.S.A.

DEDICATION

To my parents,
James and Kathryn,
who taught me the
benefits of physical activity
at an early age.

Photography by: Joseph C. Antinarella

Cover Models: *Models:*

Christine Roseaia   Troy Brothers
Wayne Smith   Carolyn Hanser
Claudine Swift   Patrice Hanser
                           Robert Hucke
                           Frank Mallia

Photos on location at:

Smithtown Landing Health and Fitness Center
Hauppauge, New York
and
The International Health and Beauty Spa
Gurneys Inn
Montauk, New York

Library of Congress Catalog Card Number 84-073253
ISBN 87670-097-0

A WORD FROM THE PUBLISHER

THIS SPORTS PUBLICATION, is but one item in a comprehensive list of sports instructional aids, such as video cassettes, 16mm films, 8mm silent loops and filmstrips which are made available by The Athletic Institute. This book is part of a master plan which seeks to make the benefits of athletics, physical education and recreation available to everyone.

The Athletic Institute is a not-for-profit organization devoted to the advancement of athletics, physical education and recreation. The Institute believes that participation in athletics and recreation has benefits of inestimable value to the individual and to the community.

The nature and scope of the many Institute programs are determined by a Professional Advisory Committee, whose members are noted for their outstanding knowledge, experience and ability in the fields of athletics, physical education and recreation.

The Institute believes that through this book the reader will become a better performer, skilled in the fundamentals of this fine event. Knowledge and the practice necessary to mold knowledge into playing ability are the keys to real enjoyment in playing any game or sport.

Howard J. Bruns
President and Chief Executive Officer
The Athletic Institute

Dustin Cole
Executive Director
The Athletic Institute

ACKNOWLEDGEMENT

Thanks to Joseph Antinarella, A. Jan Beijer, James Gott and Dr. Robert Otto for their review of and suggestions concerning the development of the final manuscript for this publication. Thanks to Colleen Boeckle and Janice Woodward for their help in preparing this manuscript, as well as, the Athletic Institute for making it a reality, especially Mr. Frank Maradie.

Special thanks to Judi A. Desiderio for her comments, suggestions, encouragement and patience during the writing of this book.

Introduction

My parents bought me my first set of weights when I was 13 years old. The set weighed 110 lbs. It was heavier than I was at the time. I still own and use that set, only now I combine it with other plates and equipment that I have collected over the years. Weight training has become an important part of my personal fitness program and an important part of my life, even today. The many benefits which I have received from weight training have been rewarding. You can experience them too. These benefits will stay with you for years to come.

Weight training is like life. To be successful, you must be realistic in your expectations. If you set goals which are attainable and work towards them logically, and with consistency, they will become reality. The same is true with weight training. You will experience success if you set realistic goals. Work towards them progressively and consistently and the rewards will be evident.

You probably have many reasons for wanting to read a book such as this one. Your desire for increasing muscular strength and muscular size are most likely varied. As a teenager it is natural to have many questions about your body; specifically, what are the effects weight training will have on you? I also had many questions at your age. Now that I have some of the answers, I would like to share them with you.

I have written this book especially for you. I have written it for the growing teenager who wants to experience the joys of physical activity, specifically weight training. Hopefully, with your help, your friends and your parents and teachers will learn from this book also.

In this book I have tried to address general weight training concepts as they affect you, the physically maturing teenager. Topics such as measuring strength, flexibility and fat levels are discussed. Strength training principles, weight training routines and advanced weight lifting opportunities are also presented. Nutritional concepts and a multitude of charts, tables and photographs are also included to help you understand and learn with ease.

I have also provided a detailed table of contents so you can quickly find those topics which interest you most; although, I strongly urge you to read the entire book from cover to cover. It is my hope that this book helps you to understand the benefits and principles of sensible weight training as well as the role sensible weight training can play in enhancing athletic performance, physical fitness, appearance, and your self image.

As you read this book and begin training, keep in mind you are a teenager, not an adult. Physically your body and the body of an older family member are quite different. Because of these differences, training tactics need to be different. They need to be specifically designed for you. Expectations need to be different also, otherwise, you might become quite frustrated, disillusioned and possibly injured. The following three guidelines will help you to achieve the greatest amount of success from this book.

GUIDELINE #1

Realize that you are an individual; and because of this, you and I, and everyone else, will grow and progress at different rates. Accept this fact and strive to better yourself first; worry about surpassing others as a second thought. Focus on **your** changes in strength and growth. Do not dwell on comparing yourself to others. Weight training will be a very personal form of exercise.

GUIDELINE #2

Accept the fact that your body will be undergoing constant and rapid changes until you are about 16 or 20 years of age. These changes can affect your appearance, your coordination and your future health. There will be times when you gain strength rapidly. There will also be times when you struggle. **Don't give up!** Stay with your program and the principles presented in this book. These principles have been proven to work over the years with other individuals. They will work for you too if you are patient and apply them faithfully.

GUIDELINE #3
Stress quality in your movements rather than being concerned with the quantity of weight you lift. Concentrate on proper form during each exercise. Progress through your training regimens as I suggest. Be patient. When your body is ready, you will gain strength and size. This will occur whether you are a male, a female, an athlete or a non-athlete. If you train sensibly and consistently, the results will please you.

Finally, weight training is for almost everyone. If you are under a physicians care for a particular illness or condition, check with your doctor before starting on the programs suggested in this book. You may need to make some modifications in your program depending upon your medical history. Most of you, however, will be able to follow the principles I have presented without any changes. You will learn a great deal about your body and experience many wonderful changes.

I wish you good luck and success as you try to achieve improved fitness and happiness through weight training.

Tim Smith

CONTENTS

Chapter 3

Starting Your Training Program

1

Training with weights will be a very exciting experience. You can expect many desirable changes to occur within your body if you train on a regular basis. This means you must be consistent in your workout pattern and habits. You must follow a program which is logical, progressive and tailored to meet your needs. You must also be patient. Rome was not built in a day and neither were you. Changes take time. Through a sensible and progressive weight training program however, as this book suggests, you can and will see changes such as increased strength, increased muscular endurance, increased flexibility and a general overall feeling of confidence. Weight training will improve your mental well being, as well as your physical fitness.

Some of these expected changes are rather easy to measure. By measuring selected physical fitness components before you train and then measuring them periodically throughout your training, you can easily monitor your progress. This process will be quite motivating. It will also help you to learn about your body and encourage you to continue with your training.

These measures are quite easy to perform and are probably already familiar to you. No fancy equipment is required and these measures can easily be taken at home. The only things you will need are: a stopwatch with a second hand, a ruler, a yardstick, a pull up bar or a strong, level tree branch and a buddy; perhaps one of your parents, a relative or another close friend.

The measurements have been grouped by body parts for convenience. Follow the directions carefully when taking each measure and be sure to record your results. Table 1-1 was developed for this purpose. Table 1-1 is also in the Appendix. By cutting it out of the Appendix section along the dotted line, you will be able to make copies of it for future use. Compare your values to the values of other individuals your age and sex. Start on your training program and then repeat these measures every six weeks. This will allow you to make periodical checks on your progress.

Table 1-1. Fitness Test Results.

Test Items	Date: ___ Score	Rating	Date: ___ Score	Rating	Date: ___ Score	Rating	Date: ___ Score	Rating
Push Ups								
Pull Ups								
Sit Ups								
Sit and Reach								
Long Jump								
Skinfold								
Total of Ratings								
Average Rating								

*Ratings: If your fitness score for a particular test is excellent, give yourself 10 pts. Good = 8 pts. Average = 6 pts. Below average = 4 pts. Low = 2 pts.

**Average Rating: Equals your "Total of Ratings" divided by 6.

MEASURING STRENGTH

The measurement of strength is often difficult. Is the person who can do 100 push ups stronger than the individual who can perform 100 sit ups? Maybe the person who can jump 6 feet, is stronger than both of these people? Strength is relative to those muscles being discussed. Ideally, you should measure the strength in all your muscles. This, of course, would be rather difficult to do and would be very time consuming. A more logical approach is to measure the strength in the major muscle groups of your body. By measuring these key muscles you can obtain a pretty good idea of your overall strength levels. You will also be taking flexibility and body composition measures by following the assessment program outlined in this chapter. These fitness components will also be altered as a result of prudent weight training.

UPPER BODY STRENGTH

The major muscles found in your upper body are the muscles of your chest and the muscles in your back. You use your chest muscles when you perform any activity that requires a pushing movement, such as the shot put, pushing someone away or doing a push up. This movement also uses some of the strength in your shoulders and the back portion of your upper arms. Your shoulders and arms merely assist your chest muscles however, and your chest muscles do the majority of the work. Your back muscles are responsible for helping you in all types of pulling movements, such as paddling a surfboard, raking leaves or performing a pull up. Again, your shoulders offer help and the front of your upper arms do as well.

For years, the push up and pull up tests have been used to measure strength in these muscle groups. They are simple and safe measures to perform and also measure the strength in your shoulders and upper arms. Read the directions carefully before attempting these movements.

4

Push Ups. To start the push up test assume the position illustrated by either photo 1-1 or 1-2 depending upon your sex. Lower your chest to the floor until it touches, (1-3, 1-4), then straighten your arms as you push your body away from the floor. Your arms must lock fully again before starting the movement over. Let a friend count how many you can do in a row. The test is over when you cannot return to the starting position or when you must stop and rest. Record your score on a copy of table 1-1, **Fitness Test Results.** Be sure to rate your score by comparing it with the values presented on either table 1-2 or 1-3.

Photo 1-1

Photo 1-2

Photo 1-3

Photo 1-4

Pull Ups. Males can measure the strength in their back muscles by performing a pull up test. Find a bar or a strong level tree branch from which you can hang as illustrated in photo 1-5. Your feet should not be able to touch the ground when your arms are fully extended. Grasp the bar with your palms facing away. Raise your body from this full hanging position by bending your elbows until you have pulled your chin up over the bar. Then lower your body to a full hanging position again and count this movement as a score of 1. Do as many in a row as you can. The test is considered finished when you can no longer pull your chin up over the bar.

Be careful not to rest your chin on the bar or to kick your legs to help you up. Let the muscles of your back, your shoulders and your upper arms do all the work. A friend can spot for you by standing just behind you, ready to catch you should your hands slip.

You should again record and rate your score. Table 1-4 will allow you to compare your value with others your age.

Photo 1-5

Flexed Arm Hang. The flexed arm hang uses the same equipment as the pull up and it measures the same muscle groups but it is designed for females. Have a parnter help you into the position illustrated in photo 1-6. Once you are set, you should try to maintain this position for as long as possible. A partner should not only spot for you but must also time how long you can hang. Your partner should record your time to the nearest second.

Be careful not to rest your chin on the bar. When your chin falls below the level of the bar the test is considered to be over. Table 1-5 presents values for this test. Be sure to record and rate your score on table 1-1.

Photo 1-6

Table 1-2. Push Up Norms for Males.

Excellent	32-36 +
Good	24-31
Average	16-32
Below Average	7-15
Low	0-6

Bookwalter, K.W.: Further Studies of Indiana Motor Fitness Index. **Bulletin of the School of Education,** Bureau of Cooperative Research and Field Service, Indiana University. Vol. 19, No. 5, September 1943.

Table 1-3. Push Up Norms for Females.

Excellent	54-61 +
Good	39-53
Average	25-38
Below Average	10-24
Low	0-9

Metheny. E. (Chairman, Committee Report): Physical Performance Levels for High School Girls. **Journal of Health and Physical Education.** Vol. 16, No. 6, 1945, pp. 309.

Table 1-4. Pull Up Norms for Males.

Rating	Age Group By Year						
	11	12	13	14	15	16	17+
Excellent	7-20	7-15	9-24	10-20	11-25	13-25	14-32
Good	4-6	4-6	5-8	7-10	8-10	10-12	10-12
Average	2-3	2-3	3-5	5-6	6-7	7-9	8-10
Below Average	1-2	1-2	1-3	3-4	4-5	5-6	5-7
Low	0	0	1	2	3	4	5

AAHPERD, **AAHPERD Youth Fitness Manual**, Revised, Washington, DC, 1966, pp. 34, 65.

Table 1-5. Flexed Arm Hang Norms for Females (seconds).

Rating	Age Group By Year						
	11	12	13	14	15	16	17+
Excellent	25-79	23-64	21-80	22-60	22-74	26-74	25-76
Good	13-20	11-19	12-18	11-19	13-18	12-19	12-19
Average	8-11	6-10	7-10	7-10	8-11	7-10	8-11
Below Average	4-6	3-6	3-6	3-6	3-6	3-6	4-7
Low	0-3	0-2	0-2	0-2	0-2	0-2	0-3

AAHPERD, **AAHPERD Youth Fitness Manual**, Revised, Washington, DC, 1966, pp. 27, 64.

TORSO STABILITY

Torso stability is an expression used to describe how stable your upper body is over your lower body. Adequate torso stability can help you maintain good posture, which can help you feel more relaxed, and it can also help you avoid lower back pain or injury. You can develop good flexibility in the back of your legs, your hips and your lower back. Good torso stability is important for everyone but it is even more critical for you as a weight lifter. You will need this support and stability between upper and lower body whenever you perform weight lifting movements over your head.

Two simple tests which measure torso stability are the modified sit up and sit and reach test. The modified sit up isolates the muscles of your abdominal region and measures muscular strength and muscle endurance within these muscles. The sit and reach test is used to measure flexibility in the lower back, hips and back of your upper legs.

Modified Sit Ups. To start the sit up test lie on your back as illustrated in photo 1-7. Your knees should be bent so that your feet lie flat on the floor, approximately 12-18 inches from your hips. Fold your arms across your chest and place your hands on your opposite shoulders. With your partner holding your feet firmly to the ground, perform as many sit ups as you can in 1 minute. You do not need to touch your elbows to your knees, photo 1-8. Just rise to a position so your upper body is perpendicular to the floor at all times and try not to bounce. By using strict form in this exercise you will be isolating your abdominal muscles and these are exactly what you are trying to measure. This is also the reason you bend your knees and fold your arms. A partner can hold your feet down, time for you and count for you as well. The only thing you have to do is sit up as fast as you can throughout the test. Do not hold your breath as many people have a tendency to do. Be sure to breathe freely.

Record and rate your score by comparing it to the values presented on tables 1-6 and 1-7.

Photo 1-7

Photo 1-8

Table 1-6. Modified Sit Up Norms for Males.

Rating	Age Group By Year						
	11	12	13	14	15	16	17+
Excellent	48-61	52-68	54-70	54-70	55-69	59-70	59-65
Good	41-46	45-50	46-52	48-52	48-52	50-55	51-56
Average	37-40	39-43	41-45	42-46	44-47	45-49	46-50
Below Average	31-35	33-38	36-40	38-41	39-42	39-44	40-45
Low	17-30	19-31	25-35	27-36	28-38	28-38	25-38

AAHPERD, Lifetime Health Related Physical Fitness Test Manual. 1980. pp. 32.

Table 1-7. Modified Sit Up Norms for Females.

Rating	Age Group By Year						
	11	12	13	14	15	16	17+
Excellent	46-55	48-61	48-60	48-57	50-64	50-63	50-65
Good	39-44	40-45	40-46	40-45	41-47	39-49	43-47
Average	34-37	36-40	35-39	35-39	37-41	33-37	37-42
Below Average	29-33	31-35	30-34	31-34	31-35	30-32	32-36
Low	19-28	19-30	18-29	20-30	20-30	20-29	19-31

AAHPERD, Lifetime Health Related Physical Fitness Test Manual. 1980. pp. 33.

Sit and Reach. To perform this measurement you will need a yardstick which can also measure centimeters (cm). If you do not have one at home you can purchase one at any hardware store for about $1 or they will often give you one for free. You might also look in a sewing kit at home to see if there is a tape measure. A tape measure can be used just as easily as the yardstick.

Place your measuring device between your legs as illustrated in photo 1-9. The "zero mark" should lie nearest to your body. Your heels should be even with the 23 cm mark and your toes should point straight up. Have a partner hold your knees down keeping your legs straight. Without bouncing, reach as far forward as you can and touch your fingers to the measuring device. Notice in the photos that your hands should be held so they overlap. This will help to keep your body straight. Take 3 trials and record your best score to the nearest centimeter.

Photo 1-9

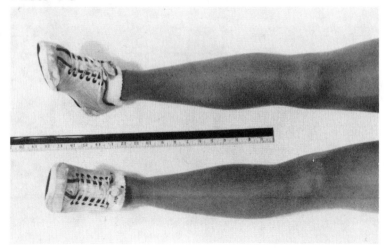

Photo 1-10

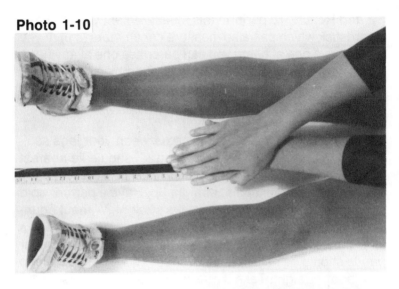

Photo 1-11

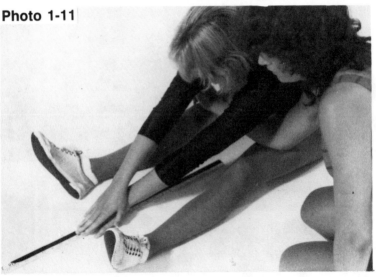

You will do better at this measurement and be less likely to strain a muscle if you stretch for several minutes before attempting this test. After you have finished stretching and measuring, record and rate your score. Norms are presented in tables 1-8 and 1-9.

16

Table 1-8. Sit and Reach Norms (cm) for Males.

Rating	Age Group By Year						
	11	12	13	14	15	16	17+
Excellent	32-38	32-52	34-41	37-43	39-47	40-45	43-48
Good	28-31	29-31	29-33	31-36	33-37	35-38	38-41
Average	25-27	26-28	26-28	28-30	30-32	30-34	34-37
Below Average	22-24	22-25	22-25	24-27	26-29	26-29	30-33
Low	12-21	13-21	12-20	15-23	13-24	11-25	15-28

AAHPERD, Lifetime Health Related Physical Fitness Test Manual. 1980. pp. 34.

Table 1-9. Sit and Reach Norms (cm) for Females.

Rating	Age Group By Year						
	11	12	13	14	15	16	17+
Excellent	36-41	38-46	40-49	42-49	44-49	43-48	43-47
Good	31-34	33-36	35-38	36-40	40-43	38-42	40-42
Average	29-30	30-32	31-33	33-36	36-39	34-37	35-39
Below Average	25-28	26-29	26-30	29-32	32-34	31-33	31-34
Low	16-24	15-25	17-24	18-28	19-31	14-30	22-31

AAHPERD, Lifetime Health Related Physical Fitness Test Manual. 1980. pp. 35.

18

LOWER BODY STRENGTH

The major muscles of your lower body can be found in your buttocks, hips and thighs. You use these muscles for running, jumping or heavy lifting movements. Collectively, this is the strongest muscle group in your body. An easy method to measure the strength of these muscles is to measure how far you can jump from a standing position. The standing long jump is an ideal test to do just this.

Standing Long Jump. You will need to find an open area in which to perform this measurement. Be careful not to try it inside where you may get hurt. It is best to perform this test outdoors on a flat open surface. Make sure the ground is level.

Make a line on the ground and stand with your toes just behind the line. Your feet should be slightly wider than shoulder width apart. Bend your knees and put your arms back as illustrated in photo 1-12. Then, thrust your body upward and forward by straightening your legs and throwing your arms out in front of you, photo 1-13. A partner can score your jump by marking that part of the ground you land on that is closest to the takeoff line. If you land correctly this will most likely be your heel.

Take 3 jumps and record your best score in inches. You can rate your score by comparing it to the values presented on tables 1-10 and 1-11.

Photo 1-12   **Photo 1-13**

Table 1-10. Standing Long Jump Norms for Males.

Rating	Age Group By Year						
	11	12	13	14	15	16	17+
Excellent	6'0"-10'0"	6'4"-7'10"	6'11"-8'9"	7'5"-8'11"	7'9"-9'2"	8'1"-9'11"	8'3"-9'8"
Good	5'6"-5'10"	5'11"-6'9"	6'3"-6'9"	6'9"-7'3"	7'2"-7'6"	7'6"-7'11"	7'8"-8'1"
Average	5'2"-5'6"	5'6"-5'9"	5'10"-6'9"	6'4"-6'8"	6'9"-7'1"	7'1"-7'5"	7'3"-7'7"
Below Average	4'10"-5'1"	5'1"-5'5"	5'5"-5'9"	5'1"-6'3"	6'4"-6'8"	6'7"-7'0'	6'10"-7'2"
Low	1'8"-4'8"	3'0"-5'0"	2'9"-5'3"	3'8"-5'8"	2'1"-6'3"	2'2"-6'6"	3'7"-6'8"

AAHPERD, **AAHPERD Youth Fitness Test Manual**, Revised, Washington, DC., 1966, pp. 37, 65.

Table 1-11. Standing Long Jump Norms for Females.

Rating	Age Group By Year						
	11	12	13	14	15	16	17+
Excellent	5'10"-7'10"	6'0"-8'2"	6'0"-7'6"	6'2"-7'4"	6'3"-7'8"	6'4"-7'5"	6'4"-7'8"
Good	5'4"-5'8"	5'5"-5'9"	5'5"-5'10"	5'7"-6'0"	5'9"-6'1"	5'8"-6'2"	5'10"-6'2"
Average	4'10"-5'2"	5'0"-5'4"	5'0"-5'4"	5'3"-5'6"	5'4"-5'7"	5'4"-5'7"	5'5"-5'0"
Below Average	4'6"-4'9"	4'7"-4'11"	4'6"-5'0"	4'9"-5'1"	4'10"-5'3"	4'11"-5'3'	5'0"-5'3"
Low	2'11"-4'4"	2'11"-4'5"	2'11"-4'6"	3'0"-4'8"	2'11"-4'8"	3'2"-4'10"	3'0"-4'10"

AAHPERD, AAHPERD Youth Fitness Test Manual, Revised, Washington, DC., 1966, pp. 37, 64.

BODY COMPOSITION

Another fitness component which will be affected by weight training is your weight distribution. You can readily tell how much you weigh by looking at a scale but what is your weight made of up? Is it mostly fat? Is it muscle, or perhaps bone? In reality, your body weight is a combination of all three components: fat, muscle and bone. Depending upon how active you are, how much you eat and how fast you are growing, the distribution of these three variables can and will change. Therefore, it is important to measure your fat content and to make sure that most of the weight you are gaining is comprised of muscle and bone.

Weight, comprised of muscle and bone, is referred to as lean body weight (LBW). Through a weight training program your body will gain muscle mass. This is also a part of the growing process. By maturing, you will also increase the density of your bones. The combination of this increased muscle mass and increased bone density will help you to gain weight and become more muscular. By measuring your fat folds you can make sure that your weight gain is the result of good weight and not fat.

You can measure your fat folds with a simple test called a "Skinfold Test". To do this you will need the help of a friend one more time and you will also need a ruler which can measure millimeters (mm), photo 1-14.

Skinfold Test. You can measure the fat fold of your upper arm by following these six steps.

1) Hang your right arm down to your side.
2) Have a friend locate the point midway between your shoulder and elbow, on the back of your arm.
3) Your friend should pinch a fold of skin and fat at this point. It is easiest if your friend uses his thumb and forefinger to do this. The skin and fat should be pulled away from the muscle. This technique will take practice so let your friend try it several times on your other arm.

22

4) Using the ruler, your friend should measure the thickness of the skinfold to the nearest millimeter (mm). Measure the distance between the thumb and the forefinger without pressing the ruler against the skin.
5) Several measures should be taken until two agree. Be sure your friend releases your skin after each measurement.
6) Record your score and rate it with those presented in tables 1-12 and 1-13.

Photo 1-14

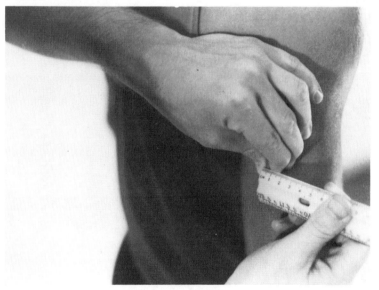

Table 1-12. Skinfold Norms (mm) for Males.

	Age Group By Year						
Rating	11	12	13	14	15	16	17+
Excellent	6-5	6-5	5-4	5-4	5-4	5-4	5-4
Good	7	7	7	6	6	6	6
Average	10	9	9	8	8	8	8
Below Average	14	13	13	12	11	11	11
Low	22-19	23-20	23-19	21-17	21-16	20-16	10-16

AAHPERD, Lifetime Health Related Physical Fitness Test Manual. 1980. pp. 31.

Table 1-13. Skinfold Norms (mm) for Females.

Rating	Age Group By Year						
	11	12	13	14	15	16	17+
Excellent	10-11	12-10	12-11	14-12	15-13	16-13	17-14
Good	14	15	17	18	19	19	20
Average	19	19	20	23	25	25	27
Below Average	25	27	29	32	34	36	37
Low	43-35	49-41	51-43	52-43	58-49	59-49	59-48

AAHPERD, **Lifetime Health Related Physical Fitness Test Manual**. 1980. pp. 31.

SUMMARY

Add up your ratings for each measurement and average them. This number will give you your overall fitness rating for strength, muscular endurance, lower back flexibility and body composition. When you perform periodic re-evaluations you should try to improve upon this average until it is a perfect 10. You should also try to improve each individual score, even if a particular score is already in the excellent range. Through this process of recording and re-evaluating you will be able to monitor your progress. When you see the improvements you will feel good about yourself and good about weight training.

Furthermore, people will tell you that you look taller and leaner. Your muscles will feel more firm and your walk will become more lively. You will feel less tired during the day and sleep better at night. A prudent weight training program will be of benefit to you mentally as well as physically.

The rewards of such a program are just waiting for you. It's up to you to go and get them!

Weight Training Principles 2

As with any aspect of life, there are certain basic principles which, when followed, will make the road to success much easier and quicker. Weight training is no different. The principles of weight training are simple and few. By understanding them and using them, you will be able to get more out of your weight training program; you will be able to reap maximum benefits for your efforts.

OVERLOAD

The most basic principle in weight training is the principle of **overload.** The overload principle simply means, making your muscles work harder than they normally do. When you **overload** your muscles in a regular, consistent and progressive manner, they will respond by becoming stronger. As time goes by and you continue to train, you will need to add more and more weight to the bar in order to keep overloading your musculature. This progressive increase in weight leads us to the principle of progression.

PROGRESSION

The principle of **progression** refers to any systematic program or schedule which continues to overload your muscles. Weight training programs are usually constructed to overload the muscles in a manner whereby strength gains are noticeable every 3 to 4 workouts. This becomes possible through the manipulation of exercises, repetitions, sets and rest breaks.

An **exercise** can be defined as any specific movement which stimulates specific, selected muscles. Workouts should consist of exercises which stimulate all the major muscle groups.

When a particular exercise movement, a push up for example, is performed from start to finish, this is referred to as a **repetition.** Several repetitions are usually performed in succession during weight training exercises.

The grouping of several successive repetitions together is referred to as a **set.** During a given workout, several sets of each exercise are usually performed.

Rest breaks should be taken between sets so your muscles have time to recover before working again. Generally, a rest period of 60 seconds is sufficient time in which to recover.

There are a variety of methods for overloading muscles during a given workout period. Some of the earlier experiments in this area developed a progression whereby individuals performed 3 sets of each exercise using a resistance which they could perform 10 repetitions with for the final set. The first set used ½ that amount of resistance and the second set used ¾ that amount. All three sets consisted of 10 reps.

Other scientists have found that 3-12 repetitions will increase strength if sufficient resistances and sets are used.

Table 2-1 presents another form of progression in repetitions and resistance which systematically overloads the muscles. Notice the increase in repetitions that took place up until week 3, day 2. These changes indicate that strength changes took place. To continue to gain strength, the trainee needed to increase the overload. This was accomplished by adding 5 lbs. to the resistance. The progression in repetitions was then started over. This process of increasing repetitions and then weight is a common and successful format for progressive overloading in weight training. It is the method I recommend for you.

Table 2-1. A Training Progression Example.

	Week 1	Week 2
Day 1	150 lbs. x 8 reps	150 lbs. x 10 reps
Day 2	150 lbs. x 9 reps	150 lbs. x 11 reps
Day 3	150 lbs. x 9 reps	150 lbs. x 11 reps
	Week 3	**Week 4**
Day 1	150 lbs. x 12 reps	155 lbs. x 10 reps
Day 2	155 lbs. x 8 reps	155 lbs. x 10 reps
Day 3	155 lbs. x 8 reps	155 lbs. x 11 reps

TRAINING FREQUENCY

How often should you work out with weights? This is a question that has plagued weight trainers for years. Exercise should be thought of as medication. The right kind in the proper amount can be very beneficial. If you don't take enough, you can expect little change; but, if you take too much, the effects may be harmful. This is true with weight training. Research has shown that three well structured workouts per week will produce substantial strength changes. Often, however, people tend to overtrain. They feel that if three days per week is good, then four or five days must be better. This is not true.

Your body will be put under a tremendous amount of strain when you weight train. Because of this, it is important that you give your body a chance to rest and recover between workout sessions. One logical way to do this is to schedule your workouts so you train every other day. If this is not convenient, then try a Monday — Wednesday — Friday or Tuesday — Thursday — Saturday routine. Choose a schedule which will be easy for you to follow and stick to it. By alternating days, you will be refreshed for the next workout, both physically and mentally.

You may hear or read of individuals who train four or six days per week. Schedules like this are more popular with competitive weight lifters and body builders. Keep in mind however, as I mentioned in Chapter 1, you are a teenager; these people are not. They are older, more physically mature and in better shape. They have been training for many more years than you have and they too had to start off slower at the beginning of their weight training careers. Even now some of them overtrain.

Stay with your three times per week schedule. Train hard when you do train and strive for quality in your workouts. More does not always mean better; quality, means better!

SETS

You should perform three sets of each exercise. If exercises are performed with strict form, proper resistance

and through a full movement of the muscles and joints involved, three sets will sufficiently stimulate and tire your
muscles. Be sure to take rest breaks between each set. If
you are training with a partner, this works out well because
one of you can rest while the other one works. Your rest
break should last for about 60 seconds.

After performing three sets of one particular exercise,
move on to the next exercise and repeat the process. Proceed through your workout in this manner until you have
performed every exercise.

SUPER SETS

As you become more advanced in your lifting
capabilities and you get in better shape, you may wish to
try using a system of training referred to as super setting.
However, you must be in good shape to try this or your
muscles will become very tired and very sore.

When a lifter performs a super set he groups several
exercises together which stimulate the same muscle group.
For example, the bench press, parallel bar dip, and the
dumbbell fly, all stimulate the muscles of the chest. To perform these exercises in a super set the lifter would perform
a set of bench presses, followed immediately by a set of dips,
followed immediately by a set of flies, and then would take
a rest break. This procedure would then be repeated two
more times to complete three super sets. Several of the more
advanced routines presented in this book make use of super
sets to stimulate your muscles.

REPETITIONS

The number of repetitions you perform in each set
should be dependent upon your weight training goals and
the amount of weight you are handling for each exercise.
A general rule is: high reps, low weight . . . for muscular endurance; low reps, high weight . . . for muscular strength
and size.

Someone like yourself, who is still growing and maturing, should train in the range of 8-12 repetitions. Start your

training with a weight you can handle safely for 8 repetitions. Keep trying to increase your number of repetitions each workout until you can perform 3 sets of 12 repetitions for each exercise in a given workout, then add more resistance and repeat this progressive system. Working in this range of 8-12 repetitions will develop both muscular strength and muscular endurance.

After your body has matured physically, usually by 18-21 years of age, you can then start to increase resistance and work out with less repetitions. A more mature body will be able to tolerate heavy weights without injuring bones, tendons, ligaments and muscles. Until then, the benefits of such a program will not outweigh the risks.

EXERCISE ORDER

By structuring the order of your exercises you can increase your endurance while going through a workout and also reduce your chances of becoming injured. Two simple guidelines will help you.

Alternate between pushing and pulling exercises. This will allow you to go through an entire workout without feeling extremely fatigued. It will also help you to reduce your chances of becoming injured because you will be able to rest, stretch and relax one muscle group while you exercise another. For example, if you perform dumbbell presses you will be working the muscles in the back of your upper arms. This is of course a pushing exercise. As your next exercise, let's say you perform a dumbbell curl. You will now be working the muscles in the front of your upper arms while resting, stretching and relaxing the muscles in the back. After you complete your curls, a pulling exercise, your muscles in the back of the arm will be more refreshed and ready to perform another pushing movement. This will reduce your chances of becoming injured, allow you to handle more weight in the next pushing exercise and also allow you to get through the workout without being totally exhausted at the end.

Secondly, exercise your larger muscle groups first and work your way to the smaller groups as the workout progresses. Your smaller muscles help you when you exercise your larger ones because the smaller muscles offer stability during the exercise. If you were to tire them out early in your workout, you may then lack the support you need when doing a heavy exercise with your larger muscles. For example, you should do a bench press before a dumbbell press because the bench press incorporates the large muscles of the chest, the shoulders and the back of the upper arms. A dumbbell press exercises only the smaller muscles of the shoulder and back of the upper arm. If you reversed the order and did the dumbbell press first, you would not have the support in your shoulder and arm muscles that you need when bench pressing.

Finally, perform your abdominal exercise. You will need abdominal strength for torso stability when you perform many of your exercises, especially those exercises in which you lift weights over your head. By exercising this muscle group at the end of your workout you will ensure adequate support of your upper torso over lower throughout the workout and not only perform better, but, be less likely to become injured.

Examples of specific exercise routines are presented in Chapter 5.

TYPES OF TRAINING

There are several methods of training for strength: **isometric, isotonic, variable resistance** and **isokinetic.** Any of these methods will produce increases in strength. They all have their advantages and disadvantages too.

Isometric exercises are exercises that make your muscle contract (shorten) but the resistance does not move. An example of an isometric exercise would be to stand in a doorway and press your arms upward. Although your muscles are contracting the doorway will not move. (If it does, you do not need this book!)

Isotonic exercises cause your muscles to contract and the resistance, a barbell perhaps, is moved through a range of motion. Push ups, kicking, throwing, running and weight lifting are all examples of isotonic exercises.

Variable Resistance exercise devices are designed so that the resistance varies or accommodates your changing strength potentials as you move a muscle through a range of motion. This concept is fantastic in theory because it attempts to maximize the resistances you move depending upon how strong you are at each given point throughout an exercise.

There are several ways a resistance can be varied. A Universal Gym for example, makes use of a lever arm to vary the resistance, creating varying amounts of tension to coincide with your movement. Perhaps Nautilus is best known for this concept. Their cams do precisely this, vary the tension on the pulley system so as to provide you with more resistance when you are in a mechanically stronger position. Resistance can also be varied by hydrolic systems. Hydra-Gym's equipment does this, in fact, their equipment varies resistance according to the speed at which you move.

These manufacturers are representative of much of the variable resistance equipment available today.

Isokinetic machines use variable resistance but are speed governed as well. This means that not only are your muscles maximally overloaded, but the speed at which you contract your muscles can be monitored and controlled as well. These types of machines are rather expensive and are often found in sports medicine or rehabilitation clinics.

For people your age I recommend training with isotonic equipment (weight training machines, barbells, dumbbells and free exercises like push ups, pull ups, etc.) because most of the athletic and recreational exercises you become involved in are isotonic movements. Since training is very specific to your muscular and nervous system development, it makes sense to train muscles and nerves the way they will be used.

SUMMARY
The following guidelines and principles will help you to train safely and successfully until your body fully matures. They will ensure that you experience maximum benefits with minimum risk.

— Overload your muscles sufficiently to stimulate improvements in strength (8-12 repetitions).

— Train three times per week.

— Perform three sets of each exercise.

— Perform 8-12 repetitions in each set.

— Perform exercises which stimulate all your major muscle groups.

— Structure your exercises so you work the larger muscle groups first, then proceed to train the smaller groups.

— Alternate between pushing and pulling types of exercises.

— Perform all of your abdominal exercises at the end of your workout session.

— Train isotonically, following the progressive routines outlined in Chapter 5.

— Perform each exercise movement strictly, moving slowly, under control and using proper form. Do not sacrifice proper technique for heavy weights. This

slow rate of movement will stimulate your muscles as they contract (shorten) which is called a **concentric contraction.** It will also stimulate your muscles as they lengthen, or during an **eccentric contraction.** Remember, quality not quantity.
— Enjoy yourself! Be patient and consistent in your training habits.

Workout Considerations 3

There are certain considerations which must be taken into account, before you start actually working out. For example, where are you going to train? Will the area be safe? Will it adequately meet your needs? Are you going to use spotters or a training partner? How should you dress for maximum benefits and safety? What will you do if there is an accident? How and why should you warm up before you train? All of these questions need to be answered prior to training, so that your actual training sessions will be safe and productive. This chapter addresses these considerations.

SELECTING A TRAINING AREA
A good training area is one that is clean, provides adequate space for your equipment and is free of objects, (tables, dressers, lawn mowers, etc.) which might get in your way if you lose your balance or drop a weight. Often when people train at home they select an area such as their basement, garage or even bedroom to store and use their weights. This could be quite dangerous if time is not taken to clear the area adequately. Plan ahead and select an area which is clean, open and well ventilated so you do not become overly hot or cold.

TRAINING PARTNERS AND SPOTTERS
It is always best to train with a friend or several friends. Having other people to train with on a regular basis will be

very motivating for you. They can offer encouragement to you; workouts will become a little more competitive because you will always want to do your best. Your training partner can also serve as a spotter, which makes sense from a safety standpoint, but will also give you confidence in trying for that last, extra, repetition.

Your training partner can also serve as a coach for you by watching your lifting form and helping you to maintain quality in your workouts. You can coach them too and this will help you to learn and get the proper amount of rest between sets.

EQUIPMENT SELECTION

Training on equipment that is sturdy, well built and well maintained is critical for insuring your safety. Most weight training equipment is rather inexpensive to purchase and is really a good buy because it will last you a lifetime. As I mentioned in the introduction, I still have and use equipment which was given to me nineteen years ago. Good equipment is also easy to find. Most sporting goods stores carry a wide variety of weight training accessories. Often you can get good buys when they run sales and you can always ask for weight training equipment as gifts.

Makeshift equipment, although cheaper to build and often well intended, does not hold up to repeated stresses as well as manufactured devices. Often these makeshift devices can break or give way without much warning. It is well worth it to purchase and use better built brand name, benches and squat racks. Good equipment will allow you to train properly and with confidence.

PROPER DRESS

When you dress for a workout select an outfit which will allow you to freely perform your training movements. Tight, restrictive clothing will hinder you in performing quality movements. You should also select clothing which will prevent your muscles from cooling off between exercises. This may mean wearing a sweatsuit in the winter months, that can be peeled off during the workout as needed, or wearing shorts and a t-shirt if your training area is heated.

A weight lifting shoe, wide soled sneaker with a heel lift, or workboot, which offers good ankle support should also be worn during training. This will protect your feet from an accidently dropped weight and help you to maintain your balance. Weight lifting shoes and workboots will raise your heels slightly. This slight lift enhances balance, helping you to maintain proper lifting form. You should avoid wearing a flat soled sneaker without a lift or going barefoot, two mistakes commonly made by beginners.

ESTABLISHING AN EMERGENCY PLAN

It is a sensible idea to have an emergency plan prepared in case something unexpected happens to you or your training partner. Everyone who trains with you should know where the nearest phone is located. They should also know who to call in an emergency, what the phone number is and directions to your training site from the nearest major road. It would be a good idea to write this information down and post it in a highly visible place.

WARMING UP

Before each workout session spend 10-15 minutes warming up your muscles and joints. A warm up session will increase the circulation to your muscles and also elevate the temperature within your muscles. This change in your body will allow you to get more out of your training session and also reduce the possibility of experiencing sore or strained muscles.

To warm up, perform about 5 minutes of rhythmic activities which incorporate all of your major joints and muscle groups. Activities such as skipping rope or easy jogging are perfect warm up exercises. Follow these activities with a complete stretching and flexibility program such as the one outlined in this chapter. By becoming flexible you will be able to get a greater stretch out of your muscles and therefore increase your potential for strength because you will become mechanically more efficient. Flexible muscles are also less likely to become injured.

When you perform your stretching movements be sure not to bounce. Move slowly and under total control. This is referred to as static stretching as opposed to the ballistic bouncing type movements. Breathe freely. These exercises should be relaxing and will stretch all your major joints and muscles. You can of course, substitute other exercises which stretch the same areas but these exercises have been selected because they will not only stretch you, they will stretch you without putting any strain on the muscles of your lower back, an area that is often abused by improper stretching and weight training techniques.

FLEXIBILITY EXERCISES

Neck Rolls. Let your head fall gently in front of you as illustrated in photo 3-1. Slowly, move your chin to the right as shown in photo 3-2 by moving it along your chest and then shoulder until it rises just up and off the shoulder. Pause, and then slide your chin back to the starting position (photo 3-1). Now repeat the procedure to the left side. Repeat, 5 times to each side.

Photo 3-1   **Photo 3-2**

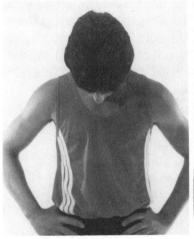 

Shoulder Shrugs. Relax the muscles in your neck, upper back and shoulders. Let your shoulders drop down as far as possible. Slowly lift them upwards and backwards and then let them down again as if tracing a huge circle. Repeat this movement 5 times backwards and then 5 times forward.

Photo 3-3

Photo 3-4

Clasp and Reach. Clasp your hands so that your fingers interlock and point your palms towards the sky as illustrated in photo 3-5. Straighten your arms and raise your shoulders upward and backward as far as possible (3-6). Hold this position for about 10 seconds. Relax, and then repeat.

Photo 3-5

Photo 3-6

Shoulder Crossover. Assume the position illustrated in photo 3-7. With your other hand grasp your elbow and pull it across your head. Hold this position (photo 3-8) for about 10 seconds. Relax, and then repeat. Switch arms and repeat the process.

Photo 3-7

Photo 3-8

Arm circles. Holding your arms straight out to the side, slowly make circular movements by moving them in a forward direction. Repeat this procedure with your arms held out in front of you and then up above your head. Perform 10 easy circles in each direction with your arms in each position.

Photo 3-9

Photo 3-10

Photo 3-11

43

Wrist Pulls. Hold your left arm straight out in front of you. Bend your wrist back so your palm faces away and your fingers point up (photo 3-12). With your right hand, gently pull your left fingers back towards you to stretch out the muscles of your left wrist. Hold this position for 10 seconds. Relax, and then repeat. Switch hands and repeat this entire process.

Photo 3-12

Photo 3-13

Side Bends. Stand with your feet spread apart slightly wider than shoulder width. Let your right arm hang down to the side and place your left arm behind your head as shown in photo 3-14. Slowly lean to the right, sliding your right hand down your leg as you bend. Straighten up again returning to the starting position and repeat this movement 10 times to the right. Switch hands and perform 10 movements to the left. Be sure you only bend to the side. Do not let your body lean either forwards or backwards.

Photo 3-14

Photo 3-15

Trunk Twist. Stand with your feet spread apart slightly wider than shoulder width. Bend your arms so that your hands touch your shoulders. Keep your elbows level with your shoulders and rotate your trunk as far to the right side as possible. Turn your head by keeping it in line with your trunk. Your hips should remain facing forward throughout the entire movement. Only your upper torso should twist. Perform 10 easy twists to each side. Pause for a moment when you cannot twist any further in a particular direction.

Photo 3-16

Photo 3-17

Knee Tuck. Lie on your back and flex both your knees as shown in photo 3-18. Slowly bring your knees up to your chest and hold them there while you stretch out the muscles in your lower back. Hold this position (photo 3-19) for 10 seconds. Release your knees and repeat this movement.

Photo 3-18

Photo 3-19

Single Knee Tuck. The single knee tuck is performed in a similar fashion to the regular knee tuck but only one knee is pulled into the chest at a time. Hold your knee in for 10 seconds. Release it and switch legs. Repeat the movement twice with each leg.

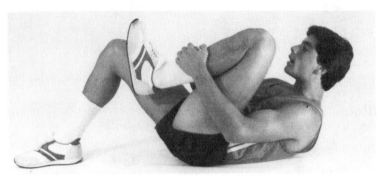

Photo 3-20

Hamstring Stretch. Sit on the floor with your legs straight and your toes pointed upward as shown in photo 3-21. Without changing the position of your legs reach for your toes by bending forward (photo 3-22). Reach as far as you can without bending your legs. Do not bounce but merely reach and hold. Stay in your stretched position for 10 seconds and then relax. Repeat this stretch one more time.

You should also repeat this exercise with your legs spread as wide as possible. Keep your legs straight and your toes pointed up. Stretch first down between your legs (photo 3-23) and then down onto each individual leg (photos 3-24 and 3-25). Hold each stretch for 10 seconds and repeat the movement twice in each position.

Photo 3-21

47

Photo 3-22

Photo 3-23

Photo 3-24

Photo 3-25

Groin Stretch. Sit in the position illustrated by photo 3-26. Pull your heels in towards your groin. Using your elbows, press your knees down towards the ground. By leaning forward your groin will get an even greater stretch. Hold the stretch for 10 seconds, relax, and then repeat.

Photo 3-26

Photo 3-27

Quadricep Stretch. Stand against a wall, facing it. Grasp your left foot with your left hand as shown in photo 3-28. Pull your leg up and back (photo 3-29). Hold this position for 10 seconds. Switch legs and repeat. Perform this movement again with each leg.

Photo 3-28

Photo 3-29

Calve Stretch. Place both of your hands against a wall as shown in photo 3-30; your legs should be extended out behind you so your weight rests on your toes. Press your left heel to the ground so that your calve muscle becomes stretched. Hold the stretch for 10 seconds and then switch legs. Perform this movement twice with each leg.

Photo 3-30

Photo 3-31

SUMMARY

Take the time to prepare properly for your workouts. The extra few steps involved are well worth the effort since you will be able to train harder and more safely, with greater motivation and confidence. The following guidelines will serve as a checklist for your pre-workout preparation:

— Select a training area that is clean, neatly organized, free from potential hazards and well ventilated.

— Train with a partner. This will help to motivate you, give you confidence as they spot for you, and help you to maintain quality in your workouts, as they watch and critique your form. It will also ensure adequate rest breaks between sets.

— Use quality equipment. Do not attempt to build makeshift equipment of your own.

— Dress in exercise clothing that allows freedom in your movements, yet keeps your muscles adequately warmed. Wear shoes which provide you with good support.

— Establish an emergency plan.

— Take the time to warm up before actually training. Be sure to stretch all your major joints and muscles. Stretch by rotating joints slowly and fully. Do not bounce when you stretch your muscles; reach into a stretched position and then hold for 10 seconds.

Weight Training Exercises and Routines

This chapter contains sample weight lifting exercises and suggested, progressive routines for the beginner.

Look at the photographs for each exercise and read the accompanying directions. It is important to lift properly if you want to get the most results for your efforts. Perform each movement under control. Stretch your muscles at both the start and the finish of each repetition. Perform each movement fully. Do not bounce, swing or cheat. Always move slowly and control the weight. You are in charge!

Beginning, intermediate and advanced level exercises are presented. By following the suggested routines at the end of the chapter you will be able to progress naturally and safely. Change routines every six weeks until you have performed them all. At that time, you can create your own routines but remember to train all your major muscle groups, not just your favorite exercises.

Although exercises are presented by muscle groups, you may actually use several muscle groups when performing a given exercise. Exercises are therefore grouped by the major muscle group which is stimulated.

Breathe freely when you perform these exercises. You should breathe in, during the relaxation phase of each repetition and breathe out, during the work phase. For example, when you perform a bench press you should breathe in as you lower the bar to your chest and breathe out as you press.

Avoid holding your breath as this could cause you to pass out.

Remember, quality training techniques will lead to quality results!

EXERCISES

LEGS

Squats. (Thighs and buttocks). Place the bar across the back of your shoulders at the base of your neck. Space your hands evenly on the bar for balance. Your feet should be slightly wider than shoulder width apart. Lower yourself until your thighs are parallel to the floor, then return to a standing position. Do not bounce but move slowly and under control. Keep your back straight and your head up throughout the movement.

Photo 4-1

Photo 4-2

Leg Press. (Thighs and buttocks). Adjust the chair so that your legs are at a right angle (90°) as shown in photo 4-3. Place your feet firmly against the pedals. Keep your buttocks and back pressed firmly down into the chair. Hold on to the handles at the side of the chair for extra balance and support. Straighten your legs until they are fully extended but not locked. Lower the weights and repeat. Do not let the weights slam down, but rather, control them and let them touch lightly.

Photo 4-3

Photo 4-4

Leg Extension. (Thighs). In a sitting position, place your feet behind the roller pads, point your toes back towards you and drape your lower legs so your knees are snug against the table. Keeping your back straight, straighten your legs. Pause. Lower the resistance and repeat. If you are using weight boots (photo 4-7) you can perform this exercise with one leg at a time.

Photo 4-5

Photo 4-6

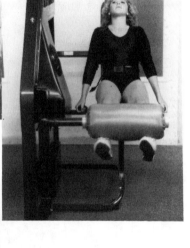

Photo 4-7

Leg Curl. (Thighs). Lie face down on the table and place your heels under the roller pads with your toes pointed downward. Your knees should be positioned so they are just off the table. Contract the muscles in your buttocks and press your hips downward into the table. Keep them there throughout the exercise. Curl your legs until the roller pads touch your buttocks. Pause. Lower the resistance until the weights lightly touch, and then repeat. If you are wearing weight boots as illustrated in photo 4-10, you can perform this exercise with one leg at a time.

Photo 4-8

Photo 4-9

Photo 4-10

Toe Raise. (Lower Leg). Place a barbell across the back of your shoulders (photo 4-11) or across your thighs (photo 4-12). Elevate your toes by placing them on a 2 by 4'' wood strip or two barbell plates. Raise up onto your toes and pause. Then lower your heels to the ground and repeat.

Photo 4-11

Photo 4-12

Photo 4-13

CHEST

Bench Press. (Chest, shoulders, upper arms). Lie on your bench as illustrated in photo 4-14. Notice your knees should be bent at right angles (90°) and your feet should be placed firmly on the ground. Your lower back and buttocks should be pressed down into the bench throughout the entire exercise movements. Grasp the bar where your hands feel most comfortable. This will probably be slightly wider than shoulder width apart. Lower the bar to your chest, pause, and then press it up until your arms straighten. Repeat. Be careful to move slowly and under control. Do not bounce the bar off your chest but merely touch it lightly to your chest. **You should always use a spotter for this exercise!**

Photo 4-14

Photo 4-15

Incline Press. (Chest, shoulders and upper arm). This exercise is very similar to the bench press. The major difference is the angle of the bench. By angling the bench at about 45° the upper chest becomes stimulated more than during the regular bench press. You can either use dumbbells or a barbell for this exercise. Grasp the barbell or dumbbells so your hands are spaced slightly wider than shoulder width apart.

Photo 4-16

Photo 4-17

Pull Overs. (Chest, shoulders, back). Lie flat on your bench as shown in photo 4-18. Bend your knees at right angles (90°) and place your feet firmly on the ground. Your buttocks and lower back should again be pressed down against the bench. Bend your arms slightly and reach back grasping the bar just slightly wider than shoulder width apart. Pull the bar up over your chest, pause, and then return it to the floor. Move slowly so that you give the muscles in your chest a good stretch. Use a weight light enough so that you do not need to cheat by bending your elbows.

Photo 4-18

Photo 4-19

59

Dumbbell Flies. (Chest and shoulders). Lie flat on your bench with a dumbbell in each hand. Bend your elbows slightly. Lower the dumbbells down to your side, just lower than the bench, until you get a good stretch in your chest muscles. Bring the dumbbells up towards each other stopping when they line up over your shoulders. This position will maintain tension in your chest muscles. Lower the dumbbells and repeat the movement. (If this exercise is performed on the incline bench it will stimulate your upper chest muscles.)

Photo 4-20

Photo 4-21

Parallel Bar Dips. (Chest, shoulders, upper arm). This is a fantastic upper body exercise, especially for the lower chest muscles. Using two parallel bars which are slightly wider than your shoulders, support yourself with your arms straight. Lean slightly forward throughout the exercise. Lower your body until your shoulders almost touch the bars. Pause. Press yourself back up into a straight arm support and then repeat the exercise again.

As you get stronger you may need to add resistance to your body when you perform this movement. Simply hang an extra barbell plate from your waist as you do your dips.

Photo 4-22

Photo 4-23

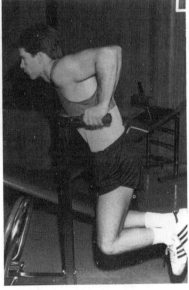

BACK

Bent Over Rowing. (Back and upper arm). Stand with your feet slightly wider than shoulder width apart. Bend your knees slightly. Your upper torso should be parallel to the ground. Grasp the bar slightly wider than shoulder width and pull it up towards you until it touches your chest. Pause. Then lower the bar and repeat. Do not jerk the weight up by using your body; only use the muscles of your back and arms. Move the weight slowly and under control. This exercise can also be performed with a dumbbell, exercising one arm at a time.

Photo 4-24

Photo 4-25

Seated Row. (Back and upper arms). Sit with your legs extended, back straight. You should sit far enough away from the weight machine so that there is constant tension on the cable. Hold the cable handles or bar about shoulder width apart. Pull the cable into your stomach without letting your upper body lean either forward or backward. Only use the muscles in your back and upper arms. Pause when the cable handles or bar touches your stomach. Let your arms stretch out again and repeat the movement.

Photo 4-26

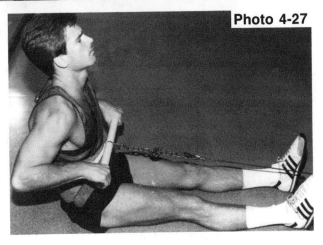

Photo 4-27

Lat Pulldown. (Back and shoulders). To start this exercise, grasp the bar as wide as possible. Kneel or sit down so that you keep tension on the cable when your arms are fully extended. Pull the bar down behind your neck until it touches the top of your shoulders. Pause. Let your arms stretch out again until they are fully extended and repeat. You may need to have a partner hold you down when you perform this exercise so the weights do not pull you off the floor.

Photo 4-28

Photo 4-29

Pull Ups. (Back and shoulders). Grasp the pull up bar with your palms facing away from you. Hang in a fully extended position (photo 4-30). Pull your body upwards until either your chin clears the bar (photo 4-31) or until the back of your neck touches the bar (photo 4-32). Pause. Lower yourself to full extension again and repeat. By alternating your touch positions, either chin or neck, and changing the width of your grip, you can develop your back muscles from a wide variety of angles. As you get stronger, you may also want to hang weights from your body for added resistance as you did with your parallel bar dips.

Photo 4-30

Photo 4-31

Photo 4-32

Shoulder Shrugs. (Back). Grasp two dumbbells with your palms facing in. Let them hang at your side as shown in photo 4-33. Using only the muscles in your upper back, pull your shoulders up towards your ears. Pause. Lower your shoulders and repeat.

Photo 4-33

Photo 4-34

Upright Rowing. (Back and upper arms). Hold the barbell using a grip which is slightly less than shoulder width. Pull the bar up towards your chin until your thumbs touch your armpits. Do not use your body to jerk the weight up; use only the muscles of your back and upper arms. When the bar has been fully raised, pause. Lower the bar and repeat.

Photo 4-35   **Photo 4-36**

Back Hyperextension. (Back). This is a two part exercise and will require the help of a training partner if you are to perform it correctly. Lie on the floor face down with your hands clasped behind your head. Have your partner hold your lower legs down. Slowly raise your chest and chin off the floor while keeping your hips pressed firmly to the ground. Pause in this raised position, then lower your body and repeat.

The second part of this exercise requires that your partner hold your shoulders down (photo 4-38). Perform this portion of the exercise with one leg at a time. Tighten up the buttock of your right leg and with your right leg fully extended and straightened, lift it off the floor as high as possible. Your hips should again be pressed against the floor. Pause when you have it fully lifted, then lower and repeat this movement with the same leg. After you have finished with your right leg, switch and exercise your left side.

Photo 4-37

Photo 4-38

67

SHOULDERS

Standing Military Press. (Shoulders and upper arms). Bring the barbell to a position where it rests on the upper portion of your chest as shown in photo 4-39. Grasp the bar with your hands slightly wider than shoulder width apart. Press the bar upwards over your head until your arms are fully extended. Lower the bar to the top of your shoulders and press again. Be sure you let the muscles of your shoulders and upper arms do the work. Do not use the muscles of your legs to help you get the weight up. Keep your back straight throughout the entire movement.

This exercise may also be performed in a sitting position using either dumbbells or a barbell (photos 4-41 — 4-44). You may also desire to exercise your muscles from a slightly different angle by bringing the bar down behind your neck as illustrated in photo 4-44. This is referred to as a posterior press.

Photo 4-39   Photo 4-40

Photo 4-41

Photo 4-42

Photo 4-43

Photo 4-44

Lateral Dumbbell Raise. (Shoulders). Stand or sit with a dumbbell in each hand, arms hanging down, palms turned in. Slightly bend your elbow. Using your shoulder muscles to raise your arms, bring the dumbbells up over your head until they are straight above your shoulders. Pause. Then lower the dumbbells and repeat.

Photo 4-45   **Photo 4-46**

Forward Dumbbell Raise. (Shoulders). This exercise is similar to the lateral dumbbell raise except the dumbbells are brought to the overhead position by bringing the dumbbells up in front of the body, as shown in photo 4-47.

Photo 4-47

Bent Over Lateral Raise. (Shoulders). Bend over at your waist so that your upper torso is parallel to the floor. Spread your feet apart slightly wider than shoulder width to provide balance. Raise the dumbbells to shoulder height so that your palms are facing down. Pause in this position and then lower the weights so that your arms are fully extended and hanging below your body. Be sure to keep a slight bend in your elbows but let your shoulders do all the work, not your arms.

Photo 4-48   **Photo 4-49**

ARMS

Tricep Extension. (Upper arm — back portion). This exercise may be performed while either standing or sitting. Grasp a dumbbell with both hands and hold it above your head with your arms fully extended. Keep your elbows pointed upwards and inward while lowering the dumbbell as far as you can. Pause in the downward position and then slowly press the dumbbell back to the overhead position.

Photo 4-50   **Photo 4-51**

French Dumbbell Curl. (Upper arm — back portion). Hold a dumbbell in one hand and your arm fully extended overhead. Keep your elbow pointed upwards. Bend at your elbow lowering the dumbbell to the middle of your back. Pause in this position and then return the dumbbell to the starting position. Be sure to exercise both arms.

Photo 4-52

Photo 4-53

72

Close Grip Bench Press. (Upper arm, chest, shoulders). This exercise is identical to the regular bench press, except that your grip should be much closer together. By placing your hands very close together you stimulate the backs of your upper arms and the inner chest muscles. Be sure to keep your back pressed flat against the bench throughout the movement and also keep your feet planted firmly on the ground.

Photo 4-54

Photo 4-55

Barbell Curl. (Upper arm — front portion). Stand with your feet slightly wider than shoulder width apart. Grasp the bar from underneath and lift it to your thighs as shown in photo 4-56. Space your hands so they are slightly closer than shoulder width. By bending at the elbows curl the bar until it touches your shoulders. Do not swing your upper body to help you lift the barbell; only use your arms. Lower the weight slowly to the starting position and make sure you fully extend your arms in this downward position. Repeat this movement slowly and under control until you have performed your desired number of repetitions.

Photo 4-56

Photo 4-57

Preacher Curl. (Upper arms — front portion). Rest the upper portion of your arms on the preacher bench as illustrated by photo 4-58. Fully extend your arms and grasp the bar with your palms facing up. Curl the bar up to your shoulders while keeping your arms pressed against the preacher bench. Remain seated throughout the entire movement. Pause in the upward position (photo 4-59) and then slowly lower the bar to the starting position. Make sure you fully extend your arms at the completion of the movement. Repeat.

Photo 4-58

Photo 4-59

Incline Dumbbell Curl. (Upper arm — front portion). Use your incline bench for this exercise. Hold the dumbbells with your palms facing away and let them hang down to your sides. By bending at the elbows curl the dumbbells up to your shoulder. You can either curl both dumbbells at once or alternately curl them. Return the dumbbell to the hanging position and make sure your arm is fully extended, giving your upper arm muscles a good stretch. Be sure to keep your back flat against the bench throughout the entire exercise.

Photo 4-60   **Photo 4-61**

Concentration Curl. (Upper arm — front portion). Sit on a bench with your legs spread comfortably apart. Rest your right elbow on the inner portion of your right thigh and hold a dumbbell in your right hand with your arm fully extended. Curl the dumbbell to your left shoulder while keeping your elbow pressed firmly against your thigh. Return the dumbbell to a hanging position with your arm fully extended and repeat the movement. Be sure to exercise your left arm too.

Photo 4-62   **Photo 4-63**

Reverse Barbell Curl. (Upper arm — front portion and lower arm). This exercise is identical to the regular barbell curl except the grip is reversed. When the bar is held against your thighs, your palms should be facing your body.

Photo 4-64

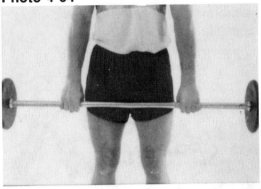

Wrist Curl (Lower arm). Sit on a bench with your legs spread about shoulder width apart. Drape your wrists and hands just off your knees (photo 4-65). While holding the bar relax your wrists and let the bar pull your hands down as far as possible. From this position curl your wrists, raising the bar up above your knees. This exercise can be performed with your palms facing either towards or away from you.

Photo 4-65

Photo 4-66

ABDOMINALS

Curl Up. Lie on your back with your knees bent at a 90°angle. Keep your feet pressed firmly against the ground and fold your arms across your chest. Curl your upper body bringing your head about halfway up to your knees. Contract your abdominal muscles and pause. Then lower your body to the ground again. Repeat this movement as many times as possible.

Photo 4-67

Photo 4-68   **Photo 4-69**

Twisting Curl Up. Perform this abdominal exercise as if you were performing the regular curl up but twist your body at the waist as you raise yourself off the floor.

Slant Board Curl Ups. As your abdominal muscles gain strength you will want to increase the resistance they must overcome. A simple way to do this is to perform your curl ups and twisting curl ups on a slant board. Be sure to keep your feet positioned as they are in photo 4-70. This will isolate the muscles in your abdominal region.

Photo 4-70

Single Leg V-Up. Lie on your back with your arms and legs fully extended. Raise your upper torso and one leg at the same time clasping both of your hands under that leg (photo 4-71). Return to the lying position and repeat this movement using your other leg. Be sure to pause when you are in the up position and contract the muscles in your abdominal region.

Photo 4-71

Knee Raise. Use your forearms and hands to support your body as shown in photo 4-72. Let your legs hang down. Slowly, bring your knees up to your chest and pause in this position while you contract your abdominal muscles. Lower your legs and repeat.

Photo 4-72

Photo 4-73

Alternate Knee Tuck. Lie on your back with your legs fully extended and your hands clasped behind your head. Bend your left leg and bring your knee in towards your chest. At the same time, curl your body and twist until your right elbow touches your left knee as illustrated in photo 4-74. Return to the lying position and repeat the movement using the opposite knee and elbow. Continue to alternate legs until you have performed as many repetitions as possible.

Photo 4-74

Crunches. Drape your legs over a chair as shown in photo 4-75. Fold your arms across your chest. Curl up so that your body twists and touch your right elbow to your left knee. Lower your body and repeat touching your left elbow to your right knee. Perform as many repetitions as possible.

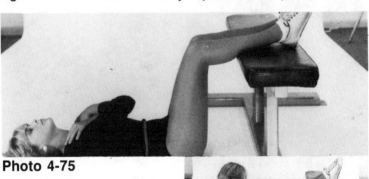

Photo 4-75

Photo 4-76

Advanced Crunches. Lie on your back and position your legs straight up over your hips. Place your hands behind your head. Curl your body up so that your elbows touch your knees. Your legs should always remain in this upright position. It might be easier if you placed your legs and hips against a wall when performing this movement. Lower your body and repeat the movement as many times as possible.

Photo 4-77

Photo 4-78

EXERCISE ROUTINES

The following exercise routines will help you to progress from simple exercises to more advanced exercise routines in a progressive and systematic manner. If your training site does not have the necessary equipment to perform a particular exercise, merely substitute another exercise which works the same body part.

These nine routines will carry you through a year of

training as you rotate routines every six weeks.

To locate photo for exercises: Example — **Leg Press 4-3, 4-4** — (the first number is the Chapter number and the 2nd number is the photo number.)

Routine #1

Exercise	Chapter/Photo
Squats	4-1, 4-2
Leg Curl	4-8, 4-9, 4-10
Toe Raise	4-11, 4-12, 4-13
Bench Press	4-14, 4-15
Bent Over Rowing	4-24, 4-25
Standing Military Press	4-39, 4-40
Upright Rowing	4-35, 4-36
Tricep Extension	4-50, 4-51
Barbell Curl	4-56, 4-57
Wrist Curl (palms up)	4-65, 4-66
Curl Up	4-67, 4-68

Routine #2

Exercise	Chapter/Photo
Leg Press	4-3, 4-4
Leg Curl	4-8, 4-9, 4-10
Toe Raise	4-11, 4-12, 4-13
Incline Press	4-16, 4-17
Seated Row	4-26, 4-27
Seated Posterior Press	4-43, 4-44
Shoulder Shrugs	4-33, 4-34
French Dumbbell Curl	4-52, 4-53
Concentratiaon Curl	4-62, 4-63
Wrist Curl (palms down)	4-65, 4-66
Twisting Curl Up	4-69

Routine #3

Exercise	Chapter/Photo
Squats	4-1, 4-2
Leg Curl	4-8, 4-9, 4-10
Leg Extension	4-5, 4-6, 4-7
Toe Raise	4-11, 4-12, 4-13
Bench Press	4-14, 4-15

Lat Pulldown	4-28, 4-29
Seated Dumbbell Press	4-41, 4-42
Close Grip Bench Press	4-54, 4-55
Preacher Curl	4-58, 4-59
Reverse Barbell Curl	4-64
Slant Board Curl Ups	4-70
Single Leg V-Up	4-71

Routine #4

Exercise	Chapter/Photo
Leg Press	4-3, 4-4
Leg Curl	4-8, 4-9, 4-10
Leg Extension	4-5, 4-6, 4-7
Toe Raise	4-11, 4-12, 4-13
Incline Press	4-16, 4-17
Bent Over Rowing (with Dumbbells)	4-24, 4-25
Dumbbell Flies	4-20, 4-21
Shoulder Shrugs	4-33, 4-34
Standing Military Press	4-39, 4-40
Back Hyperextension	4-37, 4-38
Incline Dumbbell Curl	4-60, 4-61
Wrist Curl (palms up)	4-65, 4-66
Single Leg V-up	4-71
Knee Raise	4-72, 4-73

Routine #5

Exercise	Chapter/Photo
Squats	4-1, 4-2
Leg Curl	4-8, 4-9, 4-10
Leg Extension	4-5, 4-6, 4-7
Toe Raise	4-11, 4-12, 4-13
Bench Press	4-14, 4-15
Seated Row	4-26, 4-27
Parallel Bar Dips	4-22, 4-23
Lat Pulldown	4-28, 4-29
Seated Posterior Press	4-43, 4-44
Barbell Curl	4-56, 4-57

Tricep Extension	4-50, 4-51
Reverse Barbell Curl	4-64
Twisting Curl Up	4-69
Alternate Knee Tuck	4-74

Routine #6

Exercise	**Chapter/Photo**
Leg Press	4-3, 4-4
Leg Curl	4-8, 4-9, 4-10
Leg Extension	4-5, 4-6, 4-7
Toe Raise	4-11, 4-12, 4-13
Incline Press	4-16, 4-17
Bent Over Rowing	4-24, 4-25
Pull Overs	4-18, 4-19
Pull Ups	4-30, 4-31, 4-32
Seated Dumbbell Press	4-41, 4-42
Upright Rowing	4-35, 4-36
French Dumbbell Curl	4-52, 4-53
Concentration Curls	4-62, 4-63
Wrist Curl (palms down)	4-65, 4-66
Alternate Knee Tuck	4-74
Crunches	4-75, 4-76

Routine #7

Exercises	**Chapter/Photo**
Squats	4-1, 4-2
Leg Curl	4-8, 4-9, 4-10
Leg Extension	4-5, 4-6, 4-7
Toe Raise	4-11, 4-12, 4-13
Bench Press	4-14, 4-15
Lat Pulldown	4-28, 4-29
Parallel Bar Dips	4-22, 4-23
Seated Row	4-26, 4-27
Standing Military Press	4-39, 4-40
Shoulder Shrugs	3-3, 3-4, 4-33, 4-34
Close Grip Bench Press	4-54, 4-55
Preacher Curl	4-58, 4-59
Reverse Barbell Curl	4-64

| Crunches | 4-75, 4-76 |
| Single Leg V-Up | 4-71 |

Routine #8

| Exercise | Chapter/Photo |

(These exercises should be performed in super sets by group)

Squats	4-1, 4-2
Pull Overs	4-18, 4-19
Leg Curl	4-8, 4-9, 4-10
Toe Raise	4-11, 4-12, 4-13
Back Hyperextension	4-37, 4-38

Dumbbell Flies	4-20, 4-21
Bench Press	4-14, 4-15
Parallel Bar Dips	4-22, 4-23

Seated Row	4-26, 4-27
Pull Ups	4-30, 4-31, 4-32
Upright Rowing	4-35, 4-36

Lateral Dumbbell Raises	4-45, 4-46
Forward Dumbbell Raises	4-47
Bent Over Lateral Raise	4-48, 4-49

| Barbell Curl | 4-56, 4-57 |
| Concentration Curl | 4-62, 4-63 |

| Knee Raise | 4-72, 4-73 |
| Advanced Crunches | 4-77, 4-78 |

Routine #9

| Exercise | Chapter/Photo |

(These exercises should be performed in super sets by group)

Leg Press	4-3, 4-4
Leg Extension	4-5, 4-6, 4-7
Dumbbell Flies	4-20, 4-21

Leg Curl	4-8, 4-9, 4-10
Toe Raise	4-11, 4-12, 4-13
Back Hyperextension	4-37, 4-38
Pull Overs	4-18, 4-19
Incline Press	4-16, 4-17
Close Grip Bench Press	4-54, 4-55
Bent Over Rowing	4-24, 4-25
Lat Pulldown	4-28, 4-29
Shoulder Shrugs	3-3, 3-4, 4-33, 4-34
Standing Military Press	4-39, 4-40
Seated Dumbbell Press	4-41, 4-42
Bent Over Lateral Raise	4-48, 4-49
Preacher Curl	4-58, 4-59
Incline Dumbbell Curl	4-60, 4-61
Advanced Crunches	4-77, 4-78
Slant Board Curl Ups	4-70

SUMMARY

Follow the routines outlined in this chapter and you will experience tremendous changes in flexibility, muscular strength, and muscular endurance and flexibility. Change training routines every six weeks to avoid boredom and to thoroughly develop your musculature. Remember to re-take the fitness assessments outlined in chapter 1 every six weeks because the improvements you notice will help motivate you to continue to weight train.

You can also get motivation on a daily basis by recording your repetitions and weights during each workout. Not only will you feel encouraged when you notice increases in repetitions and weight, but you will also be able to quickly see how many repetitions you need in a particular exercise to increase for that day or set. Table 4-1 was designed for this purpose. This chart will allow you to record your exercises, as well as your repetitions and weight for each of your three sets, on any given day. This table is also located in the appendix so that you can remove it to make copies for future use.

Table 4-1. Daily Workout Recorder

Exercise /	Reps.	Date:			Date:			Date:		
	Weight	1	2	3	1	2	3	1	2	3

Competitive Weight Lifting Opportunities 5

The world of weight lifting goes beyond providing a means by which to train for strength. Weight lifting is a sport in and of itself. Competitions are held in three areas: body building, power lifting and olympic lifting.

These competitions are arranged by age group. The power lifting and olympic lifting competitions are structured further, by weight classes. This provides everyone with an equal opportunity to experience success.

BODY BUILDING

The sport of body building is designed for those individuals who are interested in sculpturing their muscles, much the way an artist might sculpture a figure out of rock. The body builder must work to increase muscular size while retaining as much definition as possible in each and every muscle. Symmetry or balance is also very important for the body builder. Each muscle group must be developed to its fullest capability rather than just developing certain favorite muscle groups.

Competitions are held for teenagers in this sport and you can write to: AAU House, 3400 West 86th Street, Indianapolis, IN 46268, if you would like more information concerning contests or opportunities in your area. This is the organization which oversees the Mr. America contest, as well as, the Junior Mr. America contest in the United States.

The International Federation of Body Builders is also involved in the organization of body building contests. They may be contacted at: International Federation of Body Builders, 2875 Bates Road, Montreal, Quebec H3F 1B7, for further information.

POWER LIFTING

The sport of power lifting is governed by the United States Power Federation in this country, although there is an international federation as well. Power lifting contests require the competitor to participate in three lifts: the squat, the bench press and the dead lift. Each lifter is given three opportunities for each of these lifts and the heaviest lift for each exercise is counted towards a competitors total.

The USPF currently has developed programs for individuals 14 years of age and older. Competitions are also held for teenagers on a regional basis. You can obtain further information by writing the United States Power Federation, P.O. Box 18485, Pensacola, Florida 32523.

The sport of power lifting is a test of an individual's raw strength. The lifts are slow and controlled, as opposed to the olympic lifts, which require a combination of strength, speed, momentum and coordination. You will be performing some of the power lifts when you perform the suggested routines in chapter 4. These three lifts can be performed in your normal lifting environment with the help of your training partner.

Squat. Place the bar across the back of your shoulders at the base of your neck. Space your hands evenly on the bar for balance. Your feet should be slightly wider than shoulder width apart. Lower yourself until your thighs are parallel to the floor then return to standing position. Do not bounce but move slowly and under control. Keep your back straight and your head up throughout the movement.

Photo 5-1

Photo 5-2

Bench Press. Lie on your bench as illustrated in photo 5-3. Notice that you knees should be bent at right angles (90°) and your feet should be placed firmly on the ground. Your lower back and buttocks should be pressed down into the bench throughout the entire exercise movement. Grasp the bar where your hands feel most comfortable. This will probably be slightly wider than shoulder width apart. Lower the bar to your chest, pause, and then press it up until your arms straighten. Be careful to move slowly and under control. Do not bounce the bar off your chest but pause for 2 full seconds before pressing the bar. **You should always use a spotter for this exercise.**

Photo 5-3

Photo 5-4

Dead Lift. Stand with your feet slightly wider than shoulder width apart as illustrated in photo 5-5. Bend at the knees so that your thighs are parallel with the ground. Keep your back as straight as possible and keep your head up as you do when squatting. Grasp the bar so that your arms are resting against the outside of your knees and use a mixed grip. This means placing one hand on the bar with your palm towards you and the other palm facing away. A grip such as this will allow you to lift more weight and maintain greater control of the bar compared to a traditional grip.

When you are ready to lift lean back slightly and initiate your pull by using the large muscles of the thighs, hips and buttocks. Do not use your back or arms but rather, keep your back and arms straight throughout the entire movement. The bar should start out touching your shins and remain in contact with your legs throughout the movement. As you near the completion of this exercise use your upper back and shoulder muscles to help you straighten up as shown in photo 5-6.

Be sure to keep your head up throughout the movement, as this will help you keep your back straight, lessening the strain on your lower back.

Photo 5-5

Photo 5-6

OLYMPIC LIFTING

Olympic lifting contests consist of two lifts: the snatch and the clean and jerk. In the United States, the United States Weight Lifting Federation oversees olympic lifting competitions. Meets are held on a regional basis and include participants 12 years of age and older.

The USWLF is currently designing a junior olympic development program which they hope to have implemented by early 1985. Further information may be obtained by writing to them at: United States Weight Lifting Federation, 1750 East Boulder Street, Colorado Springs, CO 80909. The Amateur Athletic Union of the United States also encourages youth lifting though its AAU/USA Junior Olympics program in weight lifting. They may be contacted for further information by writing to: AAU House, 3400 West 86th Street, Indianapolis, IN 46268.

Olympic lifting requires strength, as well as a tremendous amount of skill. Coordination, quickness, speed and balance all play important roles in a lifter's success. The olympic lifts should be practiced with a broomstick or empty barbell bar to develop proper technique before attempting to actually lift weights.

You might try familiarizing yourself with these techniques by using them as part of your warm up routine before daily lifting sessions. Your strength and flexibility should be developed for several months before you attempt to perform them with weights. If you decide to seriously try the sport of olympic lifting, contact the USWLF to find the nearest training site that can give you quality guidance and coaching. This will be essential if you are to train safely and make progress.

Snatch. To perform the snatch correctly, the barbell must be brought from the floor to an overhead position (arms straight) in one continuous motion. The starting position is illustrated in photos 5-7A and 5-7B. Notice that your feet should be slightly wider than shoulder width apart, toes pointed forward and balance evenly distributed. With the bar resting against your shins, place your hands as far apart as possible while still being able to control the bar. This will require some practice to determine the hand spacing best for you. Your arms should be straight, thighs parallel with the ground, back flat and head up.

When you are ready to initiate your lift lean back slightly and start your pull using the muscles of your thighs, hips and buttocks. This will set the bar in motion. You can add to this momentum by continuing the pull with the muscles in your upper back. Let your arms bend slightly so that your elbows ride up high. If this phase is well coordinated and your initial pull is powerful the bar should ride up to about head level.

When the bar has reached its full height you should duck under the bar straightening your arms and controlling the bar as shown in photos 5-8A and 5-8B. The bar should actually travel in a straight line from the floor to this position. Be sure to keep the bar close to your body throughout the entire movement.

The final phase of this exercise (photos 5-9A and 5-9B) requires that you stand up, keeping your body still (no foot movement) with arms straight for 2 seconds. This third and final phase relies heavily on the strength in your thighs, hips and buttocks.

Photo 5-7A   **Photo 5-7B**

Photo 5-8A

Photo 5-8B

Photo 5-9A

Photo 5-9B

Clean and Jerk. The starting position for the clean and jerk is similar to the position you assumed for the dead lift. The major difference is that in the clean and jerk you should use the standard overhand grip. Keep your feet spread slightly wider than shoulder width apart, arms straight and resting against the outside of your knees, thighs, parallel to the ground, back flat and head up.

Start your pull using your thighs, hips and buttocks. Keep the bar against your shins when starting and think of pulling in a straight line. If you lean back slightly when initiating your pull this will help to position you correctly. As the bar rises off the ground elevate the muscles in your upper back. Bend your elbows upward and outward using your biceps to further pull the bar. As with the snatch, duck under the bar and catch it on your collarbone as shown in photos 5-11A and 5-11B. Be careful not to let your elbows rest on your knees. This is illegal and will disqualify a lift in competition.

Photo 5-10A

Photo 5-10B

From this position rise to a standing position as illustrated in photos 5-12A and 5-12B. This requires the muscles of your thighs, hips and buttocks to contract driving your body upward. Pause in this standing position for a second and be sure you have your balance and a good grip on the bar. Bend your legs slightly and thrust the bar up over your head until your arms straighten. Although you may press the bar to some degree by using your arms, the majority of the bar's momentum should come from the driving force created by your thighs, hips and buttocks. As the bar rises up step forward with one leg (photos 5-13A and 5-13B) to lower your body under the bar. This requires both balance and timing as you will find out quickly when you try it.

The final phase of this lift requries that you bring your body to a standing position, with the bar supported at arms length overhead.

Photo 5-11A   **Photo 5-11B**

Photo 5-12A

Photo 5-12B

Photo 5-13A

Photo 5-13B

Photo 5-14A

Photo 5-14B

SUMMARY

As an adolescent keep in mind that your bones are still growing and forming. Your tendons, ligaments and muscles are also in the growth stage. Any consistently repeated stress to these growing body parts may cause stress fractures or an actual wearing away of bones and underlying tissue. Overuse syndromes are very common to people your age.

Once you have such a syndrome, the treatment can range from complete rest to surgery, depending upon the severity and location of the injury. If severe enough, these injuries may even cause permanent damage.

Therefore, it is important to build a good muscular base and develop flexibility before attempting either heavy power lifts or olympics lifts. You should train initially by following the routines that I have outlined in chapter 4. These routines will take you approximately one year to complete. During that time practice your olympic lifting techniques using either a broomstick or a barbell bar. At the end of one year you should notice tremendous strength changes and feel much more confident about your ability to lift weights.

If at that time you desire to lift competitively, contact the appropriate local organization to find a quality program with whom you can train and have fun.

Nutritional Aspects of Weight Training **6**

In order for us to live from day to day, we each require energy. We create this energy from the foods that we eat. You can think of this energy as your fuel supply. If you don't eat enough, you will then be low on fuel and your body will not perform well or work correctly. If you consume more food than you need for energy, you will then store this food as fat. A balance must therefore be achieved if you are to look and feel good.

Your energy requirements will depend upon how physically active you are. People your age, who are very active, will require more energy than someone who sits at a desk all day and writes books (like me). Your body uses energy to power daily functions such as:

— maintenance and repair of body tissues
— regulation of chemical reactions in cells
— breaking down and building up foodstuffs
— secretion of hormones
— growth
— muscular contractions

You can readily see why an activity like weight training will increase the demand for an adequate energy supply. A well balanced diet is necessary if you are to grow and progress with your training.

NUTRIENTS AND THEIR ROLE
The foods you eat are comprised of six nutrients: carbohydrates, fats, proteins, vitamins, minerals and water. Car-

bohydrates, as well as fats, can be thought of as the main energy source for the body. Proteins also supply some energy, but they are primarily responsible for tissue growth and repair. Vitamins, minerals and water offer the body no direct source of energy but are important regulators which are necessary in the energy process.

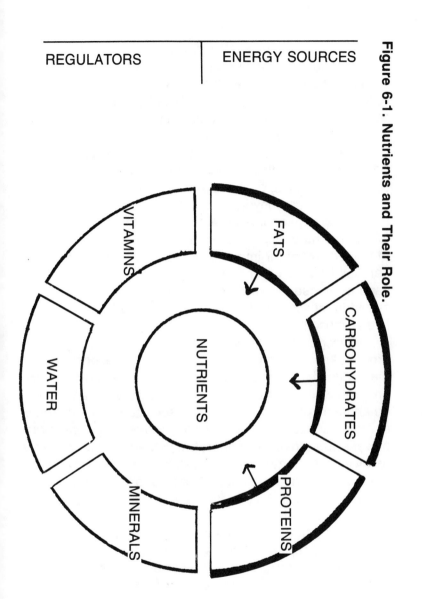

Figure 6-1. Nutrients and Their Role.

REGULATORS | ENERGY SOURCES

FATS

CARBOHYDRATES

PROTEINS

MINERALS

WATER

VITAMINS

NUTRIENTS

103

CARBOHYDRATES

Complex carbohydrates or starches are the major nutrient you should be eating. This nutrient can be found in such foodstuffs as corn, cereal, bread, pasta, beans, peas, potatoes and a host of other grains and vegetables. Not only are they a great source of energy, they seem to be unrelated to heart disease as other foods are thought to be. Carbohydrates are high in fiber which enhances digestion and they are very inexpensive compared to other foods.

Complex carbohydrates and starches are broken down to a simple sugar named glycogen and stored in your body for energy production. Some of this glycogen is stored in the bloodstream for immediate use by the brain, skin and nervous system. Glycogen is also stored in the liver to be used when needed anywhere in the body, and still more is stored in muscles, to be used when needed by those particular muscles.

Glycogen provides you with energy by entering into a process known as glycolysis. This process, responsible for the production of short term energy is referred to as an anaerobic energy path. (You have probably already learned about this system in 7th grade science.) The anaerobic energy path can provide your body with enough energy to power all out exercise for approximately 40-70 seconds. You receive your energy from this system when you sprint, play football, perform a gymnastic routine and yes, when you lift weights. Figure 6-2 illustrates how this energy path functions in your cells.

When you put extreme demands upon this system a build up of lactic acids occurs. This acid is irritating to your nerve endings and causes your muscles to ache. As a result, you usually either stop exercising or slow down your pace. This allows your body to use some of the lactic acid for energy and in about 60 seconds you have recovered. This is exactly what happens when you weight train. You use your anaerobic energy path during a set of 8-12 repetitions. By taking a rest break for 60 seconds between sets you allow your muscles to recover and refill with energy so you can perform another set.   104

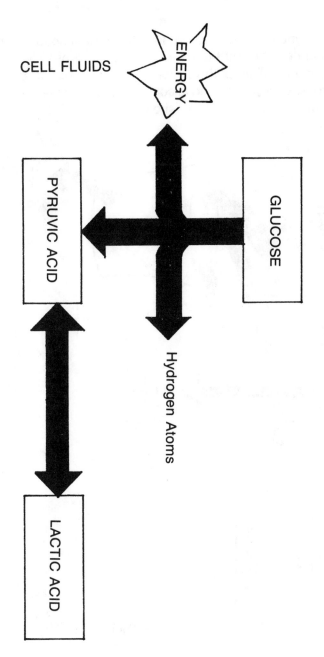

Figure 6-2. Anaerobic Energy System (Glycolysis).

FATS

If you become involved in activities lasting longer than 2 minutes you will then start relying more heavily on fats for energy. This pathway for energy is referred to as an aerobic energy path and is commonly termed the Kreb's cycle or citric acid cycle as shown in Figure 6-3.

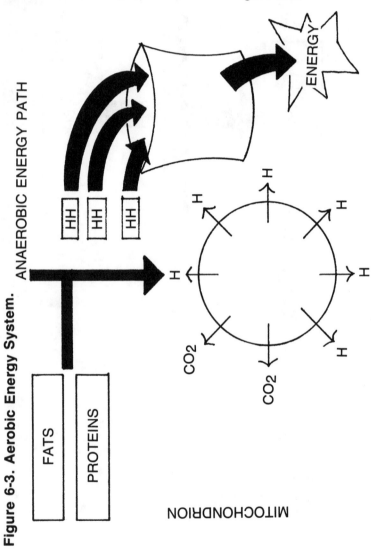

Figure 6-3. Aerobic Energy System.

Fats are an important source of energy for you if you are also involved in sports or activities of longer duration such as basketball, field hockey, roller skating and similar activities. Proteins will also supply energy in aerobic activities although their contribution will be relatively minor compared to fats.

This is not to suggest that you should also be eating large amounts of fatty foods like red meats, pork, dairy products and shell fish. There is a substantial amount of research which suggests that diets high in fats are associated with an increased risk of coronary heart disease. A healthier way to increase your fat stores for energy would be to consume a diet high in carbohydrates. Those carbohydrates which are not used immediately for energy or stored as glucose will be converted and stored as fat. Fat stores can then be used for energy during aerobic exercise.

PROTEINS

Proteins also provide some energy during aerobic exercise. Protein's main function is structural however, and only 5-10% of the protein you eat will be used for energy. Since protein is important for tissue growth and repair you should be eating quality protein in the amounts recommended by Table 6-1 for your age and sex. This recommended value does not increase with an increase in activity, nor does it help your muscles to grow bigger and more quickly. You do not need to eat a diet high in protein, as some people may suggest. Your body stores very little protein and excess protein is simply excreted. If this happens on a regular basis in large quantities, your body may have difficulty handling the water loss. You could actually dehydrate and become quite sick.

Table 6-1. Recommended Daily Dietary Allowances.*

	Age (years)	Weight (kg)	Weight (lb)	Height (cm)	Height (in)	Protein (g)	Vita-min A (IU)	Vita-min D (IU)	Vita-min E (IU)
								Fat-Soluble Vitamins	
Infants	0.0-0.5	6	13	60	24	kg x 2.2	1400	400	3
	0.5-1.0	9	20	71	28	kg x 2.0	2000	400	4
Children	1-3	13	29	90	35	23	2000	400	5
	4-6	20	44	112	44	30	2500	400	6
	7-10	28	62	132	52	34	3500	400	7
Males	11-14	45	99	157	62	45	5000	400	8
	15-18	66	145	176	69	56	5000	400	10
	19-22	70	154	177	77	56	5000	400	10
	23-50	70	154	178	70	56	5000		10
	51+	70	154	178	70	56	5000		10
Females	11-14	46	101	157	62	46	4000	400	8
	15-18	55	120	163	64	46	4000	400	8
	19-22	55	120	163	64	44	4000	400	8
	23-50	55	120	163	64	44	4000		8
	51+	55	120	163	64	44	4000		8
Pregnant						+30	4000	400	+3
Lactating						+20	5000	400	+3

Water-Soluble Vitamins

Vitamin C (mg)	Thiamin mg)	Riboflavin (mg)	Niacin (mg) (na)	Vitamin B-6 (mg)	Folacin (mg)	Vitamin B-12 (mg)
35	0.3	0.4	6	0.3	30	0.5
35	0.5	0.6	8	0.6	45	1.5
45	0.7	0.8	9	0.9	100	2.0
45	0.9	1.0	11	1.3	200	2.5
45	1.2	1.4	16	1.6	300	3.0
50	1.4	1.6	18	1.8	400	3.0
60	1.4	1.7	18	2.0	400	3.0
60	1.5	1.7	19	2.2	400	3.0
60	1.4	1.6	18	2.2	400	3.0
60	1.2	1.4	16	2.2	400	3.0
50	1.1	1.3	15	1.8	400	3.0
60	1.1	1.3	14	2.0	400	3.0
60	1.1	1.3	14	2.0	400	3.0
60	1.0	1.2	13	2.0	400	3.0
60	1.0	1.2	13	2.0	400	3.0
+20	+0.4	+0.3	+2	+0.6	+400	+1.0
+40	+0.5	+0.5	+5	+0.5	+100	+1.0

Minerals

Calcium (mg)	Phosphorus (mg)	Magnesium (mg)	Iron (mg)	Zinc (mg)
360	240	50	10	3
540	360	70	15	5
800	800	150	15	10
800	800	200	10	10
800	800	250	10	10
1200	1200	350	18	15
1200	1200	400	18	15
800	800	350	10	15
800	800	350	10	15
800	800	350	10	15
1200	1200	300	18	15
1200	1200	300	18	15
800	800	300	18	15
800	800	300	18	15
800	800	300	10	15
+400	+400	+150	10	+ 5
+400	+400	+150	+10	+10

*National Academy of Sciences. Recomended Dietary Allowances. Ninth Revised Edition.

VITAMINS

Vitamins are small organic substances which function as chemical regulators. They are needed in rather limited quantities and can adequately be derived from your normal diet if it is well balanced. Vitamins provide no direct source of energy and rarely need to be supplemented. Your doctor may have you taking a multiple vitamin just to be sure you are getting your proper daily allowance, but vitamins do not need to be taken in massive quantities to get bigger and stronger.

MINERALS

Minerals aid in the build up and break down of foodstuffs. More than likely you will consume enough minerals if your diet is well balanced. People your age may need iron supplements however.

Iron is needed for bone growth and red blood cell production. As an adolescent your body is experiencing a tremendous growth period, especially in bone development. Adequate iron intake is therefore important for your current and future good health. Your doctor can help guide you as to how much your body requires.

WATER

Water is needed by your body to transport nutrients for energy production, to rid your body of cellular waste products and to regulate your temperature. The need for water will increase during hot and humid weather and after intense workouts. Feel free to drink water whenever you become thirsty, even during a workout. You can never drink too much water.

BALANCING YOUR DIET

There are many theories on what constitutes a well balanced diet. Most experts agree however, that a diet rich in complex carbohydrates (such as vegetables, spaghetti or fresh fruits) and low in fats will not only be healthy, it will also allow you to train hard and increase your strength. By eating a variety of foods from the four groups presented in Table 6-2 you will be able to receive an adequate supply of protein, vitamins and minerals.

Table 6-2. The Four Group Food Plan.

Food Category	Examples	Recommended Daily Servings
1. Milk and Dairy products *	Milk, cheese, ice cream, sour cream, yogurt, etc.	2
2. Meat and high protein foods **	Meat, fish, poultry, eggs, dried beans, peas, nuts, peanut butter, etc.	2
3. Vegetables and fruits	Green and yellow vegetables, citrus fruits, tomatoes, etc.	4
4. Cereals and grains	Enriched breads, cereals, flour, baked goods, whole grain products.	4

* If you are consuming large quantities of milk or milk products, substitute skim milk. This will reduce the quantity of saturated fats in your diet.

** Fish, chicken, and high protein vegetables contain significantly less saturated fats than many of the other protein sources.

Table 6-3. Record of Caloric Consumption.

Date:_____.

Food	Sun.	Mon.	Tues.	Wed.	Thurs.	Fri.	Sat.	Total	%
K-Cal									
Carbohydrate									
Fats									
Protein									
Vitamin A									
Vitamin D									
Vitamin E									
Vitamin C									
Thiamin									
Riboflavin									

Table 6-3. Record of Caloric Consumption (continued)

Date _____.

	Sun.	Mon.	Tues.	Wed.	Thurs.	Fri.	Sat.	Total	%
Niacin									
Vitamin B-6									
Folacin									
Vitamin B-12									
Calcium									
Phosphoras									
Magnesium									
Iron									
Zinc									
Iodine									

You can check to see if you are eating balanced meals by keeping a record of what you eat. Table 6-3 was developed for this purpose. A copy of Table 6-3 is also in the appendix so that you may make additional copies for personal use.

Read the labels of the foodstuffs you are eating. Your parents can help you measure portion size. Record these values on Table 6-3 and add them up for each category.

You can also check to see what percentages of carbohydrates, fats and proteins you are eating. I would recommend aiming for a diet which is 60-70% carbohydrates, 15-20% fat and the remainder, 10-15% protein. If you find that you are lacking in certain food groups or nutrients discuss this with your parents, your health teacher at school or your school's dietician. They will be able to help and guide you.

Repeat this procedure for a week and calculate your daily average. Compare your values with those presented in Table 6-1 to be sure you are obtaining your recommended daily requirements.

PRINCIPLES OF GAINING WEIGHT

One of the reasons people train with weights, especially athletes, is to gain weight. Ideally, this weight gain should be in lean body weight (LBW) and not fat. This is why a periodical body composition assessment as presented in chapter 1 is useful. It will allow you to monitor your weight distribution (fat vs. LBW) as you gain weight.

In order to gain one pound of LBW you need to ingest 2500 calories more than you expend during normal daily activities. Table 6-3 can again be of help to you. Add up the values in the column entitled "k-cals" and put the sum in the box marked "total". Add up the record sheets for seven days to obtain a weekly value. In order to gain weight you will have to consume more food than you presently are, while keeping your energy expenditure (activities and lifestyle) the same.

Set a weight gain goal for yourself which is realistic. If you try to gain too much weight, too soon, you will become frustrated. A goal of 4 pounds per month, or about 1 pound per week is realistic. Do not weigh yourself everyday. Establish your weight program, train hard, and then weigh yourself about every four weeks. By weighing yourself less often you will feel better about the weight gains you see and you will also be more likely to see gains.

Figure out a way to increase your weekly caloric intake by 2500 calories if you want to gain 1 pound per week. You will need to increase by 5000 calories if you want to gain 2 pounds. This would mean about an extra 400-500 calories per day over your present caloric consumption. Look at the labels of foods which you like and figure out which foods you could increase to help you meet your goal. However, be sure to maintain a balanced diet.

One way to do this is to eat three meals a day on a regular schedule. A regular eating pattern makes gaining weight much easier. You may also need to eat snacks between your regularly scheduled meals. Make sure you eat good foods as snacks though; foods which are nutritionally balanced and will help you receive your daily requirements of protein, vitamins and minerals.

Some people find it easier to gain weight by drinking extra calories rather than eating them. Milk or milkshakes are common liquid sources for extra calories. If you should choose this route, be careful to also monitor your percentage of total fat consumption since milk and milkshakes are also high in fat content. Remember to keep your fat consumption in the recommended 15-20% range.

Gaining weight is not always easy for an active individual. By starting on a weight training program you will be even more active. Start all your nutritional record keeping about two weeks after you start training. This will give you a better idea of your true dietary habits. Once these are established, a weight gaining program will be easy to develop and follow.

PRINCIPLES OF WEIGHT LOSS

The principles of weight loss are quite simple. They are just the opposite of the weight gaining principles. You must create a caloric imbalance on the negative side to lose weight, eating less and exercising more. With weight loss, the idea is to retain the LBW but reduce the fat content.

Unfortunately, weight lifting does little to burn calories because it is not an aerobic activity like jogging or swimming. Those activities are continuous and last for longer durations (2 minutes and longer) than a weight lifting set. They therefore stimulate the aerobic energy path which will utilize fats for fuel. Weight liftings only function in weight loss is to maintain muscle tonus and LBW.

PROTEIN AND MUSCLE GROWTH

When people talk about weight training the topics of muscular size and muscular strength naturally come up. Along with these topics you will often hear talk of the Hi-Protein Diet. This is because protein is used by your body to repair and build tissue, which is often thought to be critical if you are to be increasing the tissue size of your muscles. Although somewhat logical in concept, the principle of increasing your protein intake to increase muscle size just doesn't work.

Your body stores very little protein. What it does not use it destroys in the liver. It is then transported to the kidneys where urea is formed. Urea becomes mixed with water to form urine, and then, it is excreted. In fact, Hi-Protein Diets are often used for weight loss programs. Here's why.

By eating a diet high in protein you will be consuming less carbohydrates and fats which you need for energy and weight gain. Additionally, over time, the water loss associated with a Hi-Protein Diet will cause you to become dehydrated. This will make you feel weak, tired and hot. In fact, during hot and humid weather this condition may prove to be quite hazardous to your health. These conditions are of course in direct conflict with the principles and benefits of a prudent weight training program. There is no quick or simple method to obtain big muscles. You need to train logically, systematically and progressively for a long time to see improvements. You need to eat balanced meals which are nutritious and you need to be patient.

ANABOLIC STEROIDS

You may also know or hear of individuals who are taking anabolic steroids to gain strength and muscular size. Anabolic steroids are a man-made substance which mimic the male hormone testosterone. It is the presence of this hormone at puberty, which allows males to experience larger muscle growth than females. Testosterone helps the body retain protein in skeletal muscle and as a result of this, muscles will increase in size.

While anabolic steroids have been shown to increase muscular strength and size, their side effects are quite unpredictable and many times are permanent. Anabolic steroids can stop your bones from growing so you will look deformed, they may make your hair fall out, give you acne, increase breast size in males and deepen voices and increase facial hair in females or produce other undesirable sex changes. They can also cause liver cancer and abnormalities which are not readily noticeable.

The use of anabolic steroids is prohibited in Olympic competition for these reasons. I strongly urge you to avoid their use, since the potential hazards are far greater than the benefits.

SUMMARY

Your diet will be an important factor in your training program. Follow these simple suggestions to get the most out of your program:

- Eat foods which you enjoy
- Maintain a balance between carbohydrates (60-70%), fats (15-20%) and protein (10-15%)
- Eat three scheduled meals a day

— Do not rush your meals; take the time to enjoy them
— Set realistic weight gain goals (1 pound/week)
— Increase your caloric consumption by also eating between meals
— Keep an eating diary to motivate you and check your progress
— Avoid Hi-Protein Diets and anabolic steroids
Be patient with your body and let nature take its course.

Putting it All Together 7

In closing, I would like to wish you the best of luck and offer you the utmost encouragement with your weight training goals. By reading this book and training with weights you have started a habit which can last a lifetime. The rewards and benefits can be plentiful. The path you have chosen will lead to a healthier you. Just stay on the path and progress patiently.

Along the way, there will be times when you feel great; on top of the world. These times will be quite common. There will however, be times when you feel tired and sluggish. This may frustrate you and be discouraging. You may even feel weak at times. **Don't give up.** It happens to everyone. Most often these feelings occur because your body has become bored with your current training program or you may be overtraining.

In chapter 5 it was suggested that you alter your training program every six weeks. A change in lifting routines is refreshing mentally and physically. Often, this will help you through the rough times. Signs of overtraining include: loss of strength, feelings of fatigue, an inability to sleep and loss of appetite. When this happens to a beginner, they often react by training even harder or more often. This is the worst thing to do. Instead, take two days off from training and change your program. Your body will react well to the change.

You can also become more prone to injuries when you are tired, overtrained and trying too hard. It is common to become sloppy in technique and sacrifice quality in your training during these times. Remember, quality rather than quantity. Lift less, but do it correctly.

At the beginning of your training you may experience some soreness in joints and muscles. Your body may not be use to these new exercises. Start your training gradually. Use light weights. Concentrate on proper techniques and breathing. As you progress with your training and get in better shape this soreness will go away. Any sharp pains, or pain which lasts more than 7 days should be brought to the attention of your doctor. If this should happen, stop training until your doctor says it is okay to return.

Perhaps the most common site for injury is the lower back. You can reduce your chances for an injury there by performing your lifts properly, using weights which you can safely control and by wearing a weightlifting belt similar to the one being worn in all the photographs. The belt will help to support your abdominal and lower back region. You can purchase one at any sporting goods store.

It is also important to train all your major muscle groups as this will build and maintain a muscular balance throughout your body, making you less prone to injury and much stronger for a variety of activities. A common mistake is to train only selected muscles that are used in a particular sport. While this may help you in a particular skill it could hinder you in another or set the stage for an injury. The programs presented in chapter 5 are designed to strengthen your entire body. Use them as guides when you do create your own programs.

Please remember, weights should be respected but not feared. Those who try too much too soon often get hurt. Those who are patient and train systematically will reap all the benefits. Lift and enjoy. Learn all you can. Talk to everyone you can. Read all you can. But be smart, only listen to those individuals and sources who know and understand the uniqueness of your growing body. Good luck!

APPENDIX A

The appendix section of this book has been structured so that you can make copies of them as you need to.

Table 1-1
Table 4-1
Table 6-3

Table 1-1. Fitness Test Results.

Test Items	Date: ___ Score	Rating	Date: ___ Score	Rating	Date: ___ Score	Rating
Push Ups						
Pull Ups						
Sit Ups						
Sit and Reach						
Long Jump						
Skin Fold						
Total of Ratings						
Average Rating						

*Ratings: If your fitness score for a particular test is excellent, give yourself 10 pts. Good = 8 pts. Average = 6 pts. Below average = 4 pts. Low = 2 pts.

**Average Rating: Equals your "Total of Ratings" divided by 6.

Table 4-1. Daily Workout Recorder

Exercise / Reps. Weight	Date: ___ 1	2	3	Date: ___ 1	2	3	Date: ___ 1	2	3

Table 6-3. Record of Caloric Consumption.

Date: _____.

	Sun.	Mon.	Tues.	Wed.	Thurs.	Fri.	Sat.	Total	%
Food									
K-Cal									
Carbohydrate									
Fats									
Protein									
Vitamin A									
Vitamin D									
Vitamin E									
Vitamin C									
Thiamin									
Riboflavin									

Table 6-3. Record of Caloric Consumption (continued)

Date _____.

	Sun.	Mon.	Tues.	Wed.	Thurs.	Fri.	Sat.	Total	%
Niacin									
Vitamin B-6									
Folacin									
Vitamin B-12									
Calcium									
Phosphoras									
Magnesium									
Iron									
Zinc									
Iodine									

APPENDIX B

This section of the book is designed for those of you who wish to strength train for a particular sport. Please keep in mind that no matter what your training purpose is, you should always strive to maintain muscular balance in every limb and around every joint. Your training needs will vary from sport to sport. Keep in mind that strength training should only be one part of your total training program. A separate book could be written on training for each and every sport. The routines listed in this section are merely designed to guide you.

I suggest you first train for a year, if strength training is new to you, by following the routines outlined in chapter 5 before you attempt these more advanced routines. They will provide you with a stronger and more flexible base upon which to build.

Apply the same principles to these sports routines that were suggested with the routines in chapter 5. Each workout should be started with a thorough warm up period and finish with a stretching session for all your major joints and muscle groups.

Remember to be patient. Form and quality lifting technique is most important. Your resistances will increase naturally. Be sure to continue to practice your skills even in the off season. Strength training will not take the place of skill; it will only enhance your present skill level.

To locate photo for exercises: Example — **Leg Press 4-3, 4-4** — (the first number is the Chapter number and the 2nd number is the photo number.)

BASEBALL AND SOFTBALL

These sports are predominantly skill sports. While muscular endurance and explosive muscular power is not required, good muscular balance and tonus will help to reduce your chances for an injury and help you to become more mechanically efficient.

The following exercises will help you to achieve these goals. You can perform them for three sets of 8-12 repetitions, three days per week during the off season. For the month immediately prior to your season, when you are beginning to concentrate on skills more, cut back to two sets per workout to save time. During the season, two days per week, of one set will help you to maintain your strength levels throughout the season.

Exercise	Chapter/Photo
Leg Press	4-3, 4-4
Leg Curl	4-8, 4-9, 4-10
Leg Extension	4-5, 4-6, 4-7
Toe Raise	4-11,4-12, 4-13
Dumbbell Flies	4-20, 4-21
Lat Pulldown	4-28-4-29
Pull Overs	4-18, 4-19
Tricep Extension	4-50-4-51
Barbell Curl	4-56, 4-57
Wrist Curls	4-65, 4-66
Reverse Barbell Curl	4-24

A variety of twisting abdominal exercises.

BASKETBALL

Basketball is a sport which requires both explosive muscular power and muscular endurance. For this reason, I suggest training differently during the off season than during the season itself.

OFF SEASON

During the off season concentrate on developing muscular power and strength by using the following workout plan three times per week for three sets of 8-12 repetitions.

Exercise	Chapter/Photo
Squats	4-1, 4-2
Leg Curl	4-8, 4-9, 4-10
Clean and Jerk	4-10 thru 4-14
Bent Over Rowing	4-24, 4-25
Bench Press	4-14, 4-15
Barbell Curl	4-56, 4-57

A variety of abdominal exercises.

IN SEASON

During the season you can concentrate on increasing your muscular endurance by performing more exercises per workout but you will only need to train twice a week to maintain your muscular power. Remember that the exercise of daily practices and games will also help you to develop muscular endurance, particularly in the shoulders and legs. Perform this circuit for one set of 8-12 repetitions two times per week.

Exercise	Chapter/Photo
Leg Press	4-3, 4-4
Leg Curl	4-8, 4-9, 4-10
Leg Extension	4-5, 4-6, 4-7
Toe Raise	4-11, 4-12, 4-13
Bench Press	4-14, 4-15
Lat Pulldown	4-28, 4-29
Seated Posterior Press	4-43, 4-44
Upright Rowing	4-35, 4-36
Tricep Extension	4-50, 4-51
Barbell Curl	4-56, 4-57

A variety of abdominal exercixes.

FOOTBALL

Football is a sport which depends solely on explosive power and quickness. Because of this you should spend your training time performing the power and olympic lifts. Train three times per week during the off season. When the season begins continue to strength train. Too often football players let their strength levels decrease simply because they do not have a chance to train often enough due to games, practice sessions and even injuries. Training two times per week will create a sufficient enough overload to help you maintain your strength levels.

Notice that I have varied the workouts so that every other workout starts the training cycle over again. This will help you to alleviate boredom and exercise your muscles in a variety of ways. Perform three sets of each exercise for 8-12 repetitions during the off season.

OFF SEASON
Day #1

Exercise	Chapter/Photo
Squats	4-1, 4-2
Leg Curl	4-8, 4-9, 4-10
Leg Extension	4-5, 4-6, 4-7
Clean and Jerk	5-10 thru 5-14
Pull Overs	4-18, 4-19
Standing Military Press	4-39, 4-40
Dumbbell Flies	4-20, 4-21
Close Grip Bench Press	4-54, 4-55
Seated Row	4-26, 4-27

A variety of abdominal exercises.

Day #2

Exercises	Chapter/Photo
Dead Lift	5-5, 5-6
Leg Curl	4-8, 4-9, 4-10
Toe Raise	4-11, 4-12, 4-13
Bench Press	4-14, 4-15
Lat Pulldown	4-28, 4-29
Incline Press	4-16, 4-17
Shoulder Shrugs	3-3, 3-4, 4-33, 4-34
Parallel Bar Dips	4-22, 4-23
Preacher Curls	4-58, 4-59

A variety of abdominal exercises.

IN SEASON

During the season perform one set of the following exercises training two times per week. Perform 8-12 repetitions for each exercise and super set them as grouped.

Exercise	Chapter/Photo
Leg Press	4-3, 4-4
Leg Curl	4-8, 4-9, 4-10
Leg Extension	4-5, 4-6, 5-7

Bench Press	4-14, 4-15
Incline Press	4-16, 4-17
Parallel Bar Dips	4-22, 4-23
Lat Pulldown	4-28, 4-29
Seated Row	4-26, 4-27
Pull Ups	4-30, 4-31, 4-32
Seated Dumbbell Press	4-41, 4-42
Tricep Extension	4-50, 4-51
Close Grip Bench Press	4-54, 4-55
Clean and Jerk	5-10 thru 5-14
Upright Rowing	4-35, 4-36
Barbell Curl	4-56, 5-57

A variety of abdominal exercises.

HOCKEY, LACROSSE AND SOCCER

These sports require you to possess both muscular endurance and explosive muscular power for short durations of time. The need for various degrees of strength will vary slightly from position to position but a general strength program will be of benefit to you no matter where you play.

OFF SEASON

Your off season strength program should be followed three times per week. Perform three sets of each exercise for 8-12 repetitions.

Exercise	Chapter/Photo
Squats	4-1, 4-2
Leg Curl	4-8, 4-9, 4-10
Leg Extension	4-5, 4-6, 4-7
Toe Raise	4-11, 4-12, 4-13
Bench Press	4-14, 4-15
Lat PUlldown	4-28, 4-29
Parallel Bar Dips	4-22, 4-23
Pull Overs	4-18, 4-19

Tricep Extension	4-50, 4-51
Dumbbell Flies	4-20, 4-21
Barbell Curls	4-56, 4-57
Upright Rowing	4-35, 4-36

A variety of abdominal exercises.

IN SEASON

Cut back on your in season workouts to three sets one day a week and one set, twice a week, using the same or similar exercises.

SWIMMING

The sport of swimming, unlike many other sports is predominantly a sport of pulling, with a minimal amount of pushing. It has also turned into a year round sport so there is no real off season and in season, only peak season and off peak season.

The following exercises can be performed as super sets by group. If you are off peak go through the circuit three times. As you start to peak, concentrate more on speed in the water and flexibility, cutting your sets back to one. You should be strength training three times per week and perform 8-12 repetitions per set.

Exercise	Chapter/Photo
Leg Press	4-3, 4-4
Leg Curl	4-8, 4-9, 4-10
Leg Extension	4-5, 4-6, 4-7
Toe Raise	4-11, 4-12, 4-13
Bent Over Rowing	4-24, 4-25
Seated Row	4-26, 4-27
Upright Rowing	4-35, 4-36
Pull Overs	4-18, 4-19
Dumbbell Flies	4-20, 4-21

| Lat Pulldown | 4-28, 4-29 |
| Pull Ups | 4-30, 4-31, 4-32 |

A wide variety of abdominal exercises performed in high repetitions.

TENNIS

Tennis is a sport which not only requires tremendous speed, quickness, agility and motor skills but, it also requires muscular endurance as well. The following exercises should be performed in super sets by group. Each exercise should consist of 8-12 repetitions. You should try to go through the entire circuit three times, three times per week.

Exercise	Chapter/Photo
Leg Press	4-3, 4-4
Leg Curl	4-8, 4-9, 4-10
Leg Extension	4-5, 4-6, 4-7
Toe Raise	4-11, 4-12, 4-13
Pull Overs	4-18, 4-19
Dumbbell Flies	4-20, 4-21
Lat Pulldown	4-28, 4-29
Tricep Extension	4-50, 4-51
Barbell Curl	4-56, 4-57
Reverse Barbell Curl	4-24
Wrist Curls	4-65, 4-66

A wide variety of twisting abdominal exercises.

TRACK AND FIELD

The sport of track and field encompasses many different types of sport skills. Just as varied are the needs of the athletes in different events. I have therefore broken routines down by category. All exercises should be performed three times per week for 8-12 repetitions. The number of sets and the manner in which exercises are grouped will vary.

MIDDLE DISTANCE AND DISTANCE RUNNERS

Perform these exercises as a circuit. Move right from one exercise to the next. The focus here is on developing muscular endurance and one set of each exercise should suffice.

Exercises	Chapter/Photo
Leg Press	4-3, 4-4
Leg Curl	4-8, 4-9, 4-10
Leg Extension	4-5, 4-6, 4-7
Toe Raise	4-11, 4-12, 4-13
Bench Press	4-14, 4-15
Lat Pulldown	4-28, 4-29
Seated Posterior Press	4-43, 4-44
Upright Rowing	4-35, 4-36
Parallel Bar Dips	4-22, 4-23
Pull Ups	4-30, 4-31, 4-32
Seated Row	4-26, 4-27
Shoulder Shrugs	4-33, 4-34
Barbell Curl	4-56, 4-57

A variety of abdominal exercises.

SPRINTERS AND JUMPERS

Perform these exercises as super sets. The focus is on developing muscular power. Complete each super set two times before moving on to the next exercise.

Exercise	Chapter/Photo
Leg Press	4-3, 4-4
Leg Curl	4-8, 4-9, 4-10
Leg Extension	4-5, 4-6, 4-7
Toe Raise	4-11, 4-12, 4-13
Clean and Jerk	5-10 thru 5-14
Upright Rowing	4-35, 4-36
Shoulder Shrugs	4-33, 4-34

Bench Press	4-14, 4-15
Parallel Bar Dips	4-22, 4-23
Close Grip Bench Press	4-54, 4-55
Bent Over Rowing	4-24, 4-25
Seated Row	4-25, 4-27
Pull Ups	4-30, 4-31, 4-32
Standing Military Press	4-39, 4-40
Seated Dumbbell Press	4-41, 4-42

A wide variety of abdominal exercises.

WEIGHT THROWERS

You should perform three sets of one super set and then move on to the next set. The main focus should be on strength development.

Exercise	Chapter/Photo
Squats	4-1, 4-2
Leg Curl	4-8, 4-9, 4-10
Toe Raise	4-11, 4-12, 4-13
Clean and Jerk	5-10 thru 5-14
Upright Rowing	4-35, 4-36
Shoulder Shrugs	4-33, 4-34
Bench Press	4-14, 4-15
Parallel Bar Dips	4-22, 4-23
Close Grip Bench Press	4-54, 4-55
Bent Over Rowing	4-24, 4-25
Pull Overs	4-18, 4-19
Dumbbell Flies	4-20, 4-21
Incline Press	4-16, 4-17
Seated Dumbbell Press	4-41, 4-42
Seated Posterior Press	4-43, 4-44

Preacher Curl	4-58, 4-59
Incline Dumbbell Curls	4-60, 4-61
Concentration Curl	4-62, 4-63

A variety of twisting abdominal exercises.

VOLLEYBALL

Volleyball is an explosive sport. Muscular power should be your main focus. During the off season perform this exercise routine three times per week, using three sets of 8-12 repetitions. Once you start your season, two training sessions per week will be enough to maintain your strength.

Exercises	**Chapter/Photo**
Squats	4-1, 4-2
Leg Curls	4-8, 4-9, 4-10
Bench Press	4-14, 4-15
Bent Over Rowing	4-24, 4-25
Incline Press	4-16, 4-17
Pull Overs	4-18, 4-19
Seated Dumbbell Press	4-41, 4-42
Dumbbell Flies	4-20, 4-21
Clean and Jerk	5-10 thru 5-14
Barbell Curl	4-56, 4-57
French Dumbbell Curl	4-52, 4-53

A variety of abdominal exercises.

WRESTLING

The sport of wrestling requires both muscular strength and muscular endurance. It also requires pushing and pulling skills. As a wrestler you must develop strength and flexibility throughout your entire body.

During the off season you should focus on strength development through the use of super sets, training three times per week for three sets of 8-12 repetitions. Your in season training should focus more on muscular endurance. The practice sessions themselves will help to do this but by using a circuit program of one set per exercise, three times per week, you will be able to maintain strength and muscular balance.

OFF SEASON

Exercise	Chapter/Photo
Leg Press	4-3, 4-4
Leg Curl	4-8, 4-9, 4-10
Leg Extension	4-5, 4-6, 4-7
Bench Press	4-14, 4-15
Incline Press	4-16, 4-17
Parallel Bar Dips	4-22, 4-23
Lat Pull Down	4-28, 4-29
Seated Row	4-26, 4-27
Pull Ups	4-30, 4-31, 4-32
Seated Dumbbell Press	4-41, 4-42
Tricep Extension	4-50, 4-51
Close Grip Bench Press	4-54, 4-55
Clean and Jerk	5-10 thru 5-14
Upright Rowing	4-35, 4-36
Barbell Curl	4-56, 4-57

A variety of abdominal exercises.

IN SEASON

Exercises	Chapter/Photo
Leg Press	4-3, 4-4
Leg Curl	4-8, 4-9, 4-10
Bench Press	4-14, 4-15
Bent Over Rowing	4-24, 4-25
Standing Military Press	4-39, 4-40
Seated Row	4-26, 4-27
Incline Press	4-16, 4-17
Upright Rowing	4-35, 4-36
Parallel Bar Dips	4-22, 4-23
Pull Ups	4-30, 4-31, 4-32
Barbell Curl	4-56, 4-57

A variety of abdominal exercises.

GLOSSARY

Aerobic — an energy system which uses fats and protein to create energy. You use this energy system when you play sports like basketball, aerobic dancing, distance running and other activities which require large amounts of oxygen for extended periods of time.

Anaerobic — an energy system which uses carbohydrates to power short term activities like sprinting, a football play, wrestling or gymnastics.

Body Building — a form of weight lifting competition in which participants are judged on size, shape, definition and symmetry in selected muscle groups. Weights are not lifted in competitions but subjects pose to show the judges their muscular development.

Carbohydrates — a nutrient which provides anaerobic energy when broken down. Carbohydrates are found in pasta, vegetables, fruits, cereals and grains.

Exercise — any specific movement which stimulates specific, selected muscles.

Fat — a nutrient which provides aerobic energy in its breakdown. Fats are found in beef, pork, dairy products, shellfish and vegetables.

Isokinetic — a type of strength training in which the speed of movement is constant and the resistance varies.

Isometric — a type of strength training in which you exert force against an immoveable resistance (ie: pushing against a wall).

Isotonic — a type of strength training in which your muscles contract against a fixed resistance (ie: pull ups, push ups, barbells and dumbbells).

K-cal — (kilocalorie) — the equivalent of 1 Calorie. Calories are used to measure and describe the potential energy content of foods. The higher a foods caloric value the more potential energy it has.

Lactic Acid — a by-product of anaerobic exercise and energy production which, in large enough quantities can cause muscular discomfort.

LBW — lean body weight or that portion of your weight comprised of bone and muscle mass as opposed to fat tissue.

Olympic Lifting — a form of weight lifting competition in which the participant gets three attempts at the snatch and the clean and jerk. The best score is taken for each lift and the two scores are added together for a total score.

Overload — requiring your muscles to work against resistances greater than they are normally accustomed to.

Power Lifting — a form of weight lifting competition in which the participant gets three attempts at the squat, bench press and dead lift. The best score is taken for each lift and the three scores are added together for a total score.

Progression — a systematic program or schedule to overload your muscles.

Protein — a nutrient which is used primarily for tissue growth and repair but may provide some energy in aerobic activities. Protein is found in fish, meat, dairy products and vegetables.

Repetition — performing a particular **exercise** from start to finish.

Resistance — any weight, object or pressure used to create an **overload.**

Set — the grouping of several successive repetitions together.

Super Set — the grouping of several **sets** together.

INDEX

C

D